Understanding Teaching

by

Kenneth O. Gangel, Ph. D.

Chairman, Dept. of Christian Education

Dallas Theological Seminary

EVANGELICAL TRAINING ASSOCIATION

110 Bridge Street ● Box 327

Wheaton, Illinois 60189

Third Edition

7 | 5 4

Library of Congress catalog card number: 68-24579

ISBN 0-910566-14-3

Copyright © 1968, 1979 *by Evangelical Teacher Training Association*

Printed in U.S.A.

CONTENTS

INTRODUCTION

The joys of teaching Bible truth are increased for the one who is able to communicate well. No subject is as challenging to teach, nor message as important to convey, as the Word of God. It is, therefore, imperative that the Bible teacher be prepared. *Understanding Teaching* is designed to give this type preparation to those desiring to serve in the church education program. It would be helpful for both the new and experienced teacher.

The textbook was written by Dr. Kenneth O. Gangel, an experienced educator and leading authority in the field of Christian Education. Dr. Gangel has also prepared a set of masters for making overhead transparencies, cassette tape, and instructor's guide which help the course instructor to add interest to class sessions.

This course and *Teaching Techniques* are alternates for the elective course on teaching methods. Award credit cards for either *Understanding Teaching* or *Teaching Techniques* may be submitted in fulfillment of ETA Church Ministries certificate requirements.

Many who have already completed the ETA certificate program have found studying this course in addition to *Teaching Techniques* a rewarding experience in self improvement. Considering the principles of communicating Bible truth always results in renewed confidence and effective ministry. *Understanding Teaching* has proven to contribute much to the continuing improvement of teaching in the church.

ABOUT THIS BOOK

Among the last words of our Lord on earth we find the dynamic challenge to disciple all nations and teach them to do the things commanded by Christ. The teaching responsibility of the church has never been withdrawn nor has the need for its dynamic abated. The worldwide emphasis on education has never been greater than in this last part of the twentieth century. In this context the church faces its educational task—to teach or perish! It is the purpose of this book to serve the church in its present crisis hour by helping its army of lay workers to a better understanding of teaching.

Kenneth O. Gangel

What Is
Christian Teaching

How does Christian teaching differ from secular teaching?
What qualifications are desirable in a Christian teacher?
What are the supernatural dynamics in Christian teaching?
What are the responsibilities of the Christian teacher?

"Go ye therefore and make disciples of all nations baptizing them in the name of the Father, and of the Son, and of the Holy Ghost: teaching them to observe all things whatsoever I have commanded you."

These words of our Lord confront God's people in this confusing nuclear age as clearly as when they were first spoken. Teaching has always had a predominant role in God's redemptive plan. But perhaps at no time has there been more need for competent communicators of the truth than in this last half of the twentieth century. This book deals with the principles and methods of Christian teaching. In many ways Christian teaching is no different from any other kind of teaching. Communication—the transfer of ideas from one person to another—is the basis of all teaching. Many of the techniques used by Christian teachers are identical with the procedures used by non-Christian teachers. However, the crucial difference is the added dimension of the supernatural. The fact that Christian teaching is God-centered affects its motivation, its ethics, its objectives, and all other phases of the teaching process. Similarly, the acceptance of God's revealed truth as the basis of the teacher's curriculum provides a groundwork which is again a distinctive of Christian teaching.

The topic of teaching is important to every Christian, for although he may not be a teacher in the church educational program, his communication of Christianity as a parent, neighbor, or friend involves teaching principles. In this sense we are all teachers and the understanding of teaching is of concern to each of us.

THE CHRISTIAN TEACHER'S QUALITIES

In the dealings of God with his people, the worker is always more important than the work. That is, what the servant *is* is prerequisite to what he *does* in Christian service. What, then, are the qualities of a Christian teacher? There are two possible extremes. One places the major emphasis on the intellectual capacity and the ability of the teacher; the other stresses mainly spiritual qualities. The biblical view recognizes the importance of both ability and spirituality, and both are considered in the listing of personal teacher characteristics that follow.

DEDICATION

A Christian teacher possesses genuine commitment to the Lord and to the task of teaching. He seeks to be a steward in his teaching ministry, submitting to the Spirit of God and seeking to glorify Christ in all that he does.

TEACHABLENESS

Intelligence is desirable in any teacher. Equally important is teachableness and sincere desire to learn. It has been said that when a teacher stops learning he stops teaching. The Christian teacher must continually follow the scriptural admonition to "grow in grace and in the knowledge of our Lord and Saviour Jesus Christ" (II Peter 3:18).

SACRIFICE

Earthly rewards cannot compensate for the time and effort invested in the ministry of teaching. It is a ministry of love that looks beyond the temporal to things of eternal value. The Christian teacher's motivation should be like that of his Lord, who came not to be ministered unto, but to minister.

KNOWLEDGE

The Christian teacher must know *his Lord*, and that is why he prays.

The Christian teacher must know the truth of *God's revelation*, and that is why he studies his Bible carefully.

The Christian teacher must know *his lesson content* and that is why he prepares faithfully.

The Christian teacher must know *his students*, and that is why he gives time to visitation and counseling.

The Christian teacher must know the *principles of the teaching-learning process*, and that is why he seeks training for the task.

MATURITY

The Thessalonian Christians in the days of the New Testament learned a great deal about the Christian faith from the letters and the teaching of the Apostle Paul. They also learned much from his example during the time that he spent with them. This seems clear from the apostle's first letter to that church: "Because our gospel came to you not simply with words, but also with power, with the Holy Spirit and with conviction. You know how we lived among you for your sake." (I Thess. 1:5 NIV).

THE PURPOSE OF CHRISTIAN TEACHING

In the New Testament, Christ emphasized the importance of motivation. Note, for example, the conversation with Peter in John 21:15-19. Do we understand our teaching purposes clearly enough to view our role as a parent, Sunday school teacher, or church leader as the ministry that it is? We need to examine our purpose.

AS IT RELATES TO THE GLORY OF GOD

The ultimate goal of a Christian teacher is to glorify God in all of life and service. This becomes interpreted in his teaching ministry in terms of spiritual maturity, as the writer of the book of Hebrews emphasizes in 5:12-6:1a. This passage is concerned with the responsibility of every adult Christian to mature sufficiently to be able to serve God as an effective teacher.

AS IT RELATES TO TEACHER STANDARDS

A more detailed purpose for the Christian teacher concerns the rigorous standards of the Christian teaching ministry. Just how much can a church expect from its teachers? How high should the standards be set? Teacher standards should be established and maintained in at least the following areas:

Lesson presentation

The focus of the teacher's ministry is the time when he actually stands before his class. He must seek to use valid teaching principles, proper methods, and adequate aids to effectively communicate the important truths which have been entrusted to him. Lesson presentation for the Christian teacher demands his very best effort.

Training

Every church should provide and every teacher should desire a definite program of formal training for the teaching task. While Christian teaching includes a supernatural leading of God, teaching is a gift to be cultivated through training. The clear admonition of the Word of God is to "study to show thyself approved unto God, a workman that needeth not to be ashamed" (II Tim. 2:15).

The teacher, therefore, takes advantage of every opportunity to improve his teaching ability. This will include his participation in such activities as workshops, conferences, or similar meetings planned to provide instruction and inspiration for church workers.

Visitation

The dedicated teacher knows that his ministry does not end with the class session. The "sheep" that are his responsibility must be sought when they are missing and be helped when they are in distress. Indeed, a teacher is fully prepared to teach his students only when he knows something of their home life and environment. This he learns only by visiting them in their homes.

Prayer and love
Probably no quality is more necessary in a teacher than loving those he teaches. This is not always easy to maintain, but is always necessary. The Christian teacher must constantly seek God's power for himself and his students.

THE POWER AND EXAMPLE OF CHRIST

Here is an area in which the Christian teacher differs markedly from the secular. The secular teacher is usually dependent entirely upon himself, his school system, and whatever help he can derive from the home to impress the students with the truth. Behavior change is normally viewed as the result of conditioning or a proper combination of psychological variables.

The Christian has an additional power which comes directly from the risen Lord who said, "All power is given unto me in heaven and in earth. Go ye therefore, and teach . . . and, lo, I am with you alway, even unto the end of the world" (Matthew 28:18b-20). The power in Christian teaching is the power of Christ himself, and we have this power manifested in his own example of teaching ministry.

THE TEACHING OF CHRIST HAD STRENGTH OF PURPOSE

Christ's purpose was to communicate revealed truth. He recognized his call and on various occasions referred to himself as one whose teaching was not self-initiated. He had been given a responsibility by his Father. There was no hesitancy or fear; there was no drawing back from the responsibilities that were his as a teacher. The power which he possessed was also revealed in his authoritative message, for it was the truth from God himself.

THE TEACHING OF CHRIST HAD DISTINCTIVE CHARACTER

Christ taught as one sent from God.

He Taught With Clarity

Because Christ wanted everyone who heard him to understand the gospel, he used parables and practical illustrations to present his message clearly.

He Taught With Authority

The New Testament indicates that Christ taught "as one having authority." The officers sent out by the chief priests to take Christ prisoner came back with the report, "Never man spake like this man." He spoke as the representative of God.

He Taught With Variety

One of the characteristics of Christ's teaching which was so startling to the Jewish rabbis was his departure from the traditional system of synagogue lectures. Our Lord used almost every imaginable type of teaching technique to facilitate the process of communication. He was a master in the art of maintaining interest.

THE TEACHING OF CHRIST HAD DISCERNIBLE RESULTS

Christ's ministry resulted in changed lives. Study carefully the call of the disciples as recorded in Mark 1:16-39. Here is a graphic picture of Christ reaching people and making them into disciples.

He Found Them

They were ordinary men, doing ordinary things, but he went where they were in order to change their lives.

He Called Them

Not content to let them stand off or follow, as they wished, he deliberately commanded their attention by saying, "Come ye after me, and I will make you to become fishers of men."

He Taught Them

For three years they were at his side constantly observing the miracles, listening to the teaching, accepting his personal counsel.

He Showed Them

Their ministry was to be a pattern or a copy of his own ministry. By looking at him they were able to observe the marks of quality which should characterize their own work.

He Sent Them

He did not keep the disciples to himself, but even while he was still on earth he constantly used them in ministry to others. No Sunday school class is an end in itself. It is a means toward the growth of Christians and the development of workers to accomplish the work of Christ.

In the Christian context, teaching is the communication of the living Word, Christ; from the written Word, the Bible; through the spoken word of the teacher. It includes both a sense of gift and of call. Its effective outworking calls for both training and thorough preparation.

STUDY PROJECTS
1. Write your own definition of teaching.
2. Prepare a concise statement specifically answering the question, "Why do I want to teach in church?"
3. Study the teaching ministry of Christ in John 6, and list at least five specific lessons to be learned from it.
4. Think through and list your objectives in taking this course.
5. Establish a specific prayer list for students you are or shall be teaching.

BIBLIOGRAPHY
Edge, Findley B. **Teaching for Results.** Nashville: Broadman Press, 1956. Chapters 1, 2, 4, and 15.

_____. **Helping the Teacher.** Nashville: Broadman Press, 1959. Chapter 1.

Horne, Herman H. **Teaching Techniques of Jesus.** Rev. ed. Grand Rapids: Kregel Publications, 1971.

Zuck, Roy B. **Spiritual Power in Your Teaching.** Rev. ed. Chicago: Moody Press, 1972.

How Students
Learn

What is learning?
What is involved in maturity?
What are the steps in the learning process?
How can learning be reinforced?

One of the most important aspects in the teacher's understanding of his task is an appreciation of what is involved in the learning process.

Actually, communication is carried on in a number of ways in any teaching-learning situation. The very appearance of the room or teacher may communicate order or chaos, brightness or dreariness, friendliness or coldness, or similar important feelings to the learner. We must also recognize that signs, pictures, and other symbols provide learning experiences. However, the primary concern of every teacher is communication through a spoken language. This chapter will explore what happens on the part of the learner when the teacher speaks to him in an attempt to communicate.

UNDERSTANDING THE LEARNING PROCESS

Christian teaching is concerned with the process of bringing the student to a level of independence and maturity which causes him to think and act satisfactorily in each experience of his life. This implies conformity to the will of God and a constant growth in the likeness of Christ.

THE DEFINITION OF LEARNING

Gregory, in his famous laws of teaching, wrote that "Learning is thinking into one's own understanding a new idea or truth or working into habit a new art or skill."[1] The emphasis of Gregory's definition is essentially that the idea or concept to be learned is important and the individual himself participates in the learning process. Because of his emphasis on reproduction of an idea, Gregory laid heavy stress on recitation in the learning process.

Many contemporary educators make the actual behavior that results from learning the focal point. Learning according to this viewpoint emphasizes the process of going through experiences which will establish the individual's action when he encounters the same or similar experiences in the future.

Related To Knowledge And Wisdom

"Knowledge" might be used to define the body of content compiled by an individual as he learns. "Wisdom," on the other hand, might describe how the learner is able to apply and use the knowledge which he has gained. In this sense learning could be defined as the process of growth in knowledge and wisdom.

Related To Environment

The individual cannot be separated from his environment. A child in the classroom reflects the kind of atmosphere in which he lives at home. Full understanding of the learning process must, therefore, include recognition of the living conditions of the learner.

Related To Maturity

Physical maturation is generally considered to be the process of natural physical growth, and takes into consideration inherited characteristics. There is difficulty, however, in defining maturity in general, for there are many different kinds and levels of maturity. A person who is twenty-five years of age may possess chronological maturity because of his age, physiological maturity because of his bodily structure, mental maturity because of his intellectual capabilities, and educational ability because he has completed high school and college. On the other hand, he might be immature emotionally, socially, and spiritually simply because his growth and development in these areas have not kept pace with the other levels of maturity. The teacher must recognize that while his students may possess a degree of maturity that relates to age in some areas, they may also be very immature in other areas.

THE LEARNING CHARACTERISTICS OF AGE GROUPS

Although there are general characteristics of learning which apply to all ages, there is validity for utilizing the learning process in different ways for different age levels.

Children

If communication is the process of one person speaking to another in a language common to both, dealing with children certainly implies an age level distinction in a number of important areas. Dividing children into *properly graded* groups recognizes peer influence and level of understanding.

The effective teacher will make use of seeing, touching, smelling, and tasting, as well as hearing, in the classroom. Some abstract truths will be more easily comprehended through the use of pictures or objects. These *sensory experiences* sharpen learning for children. Since children think about life as it relates to themselves, their family, and other things close to them, the teacher should be careful to use *life-related terminology*. If the child can see *present meaning* and the truth makes sense *now*, the child will grow intellectually for his learning is related to that which he can actually apply.

Youth

Interaction and immediate relevancy are key factors in teaching young people. When asked why they have left church and Sunday school, teenagers characteristically answer: "I didn't think church was very important"; or "I don't understand how the Bible means anything to me." Teenagers today want to be shown how the things which they are learning in Sunday school and church make a difference in their daily living and therefore possess practical importance.

Adults

In teaching adults (college students are classified as adults for learning purposes) the emphasis should be on *self-motivation* and *responsibility to others*. The young parent, for example, will be concerned with his role in the home and responsibility to his children. Adults must be enlisted in their own educational development, and the teacher who is successful in securing this enlistment has often done so through emphasis on discussion and interaction in the adult classroom.

STEPS IN THE LEARNING PROCESS

Effective teaching usually involves a logical sequence of material presentation. Ernest M. Ligon has suggested the following five steps in the learning process: exposure, repetition, understanding, conviction, and application. [2] While the sequence is not always the same, progress must be made from the mere reception of facts to the acceptance and application of these.

A major goal of Christian teaching is to change behavior. Paul noted that ". . . old things are passed away; behold all things are become new" (II Cor. 5:17).

When the student has learned to put into practice those things studied in the classroom, the teacher knows that learning has really taken place.

DEVELOPMENT OF LEARNING

THROUGH THE USE OF ASSOCIATION

To use Gregory's words once again, "The lesson to be mastered must be explicable in the terms of truth already known by the learner—the unknown must be explained by means of the known." [3] Sometimes this is referred to as "apperception." It involves seeing relationships between what the student already knows and what the teacher presents in class.

THROUGH THE ELEMENT OF INTEREST

Is it easier to teach a boy to play or to wash the dishes? There may be exceptions, but the answer is usually obvious! People learn best that which interests them. Consequently, as the teacher makes the lesson material interesting and attractive to his students, learning will be facilitated.

THROUGH THE RECOGNITION OF GROWTH

Steps in an individual's growth process must be encountered and mastered in a regular order. This stair-step approach to learning suggests that each age has its own normal steps, or tasks, to complete. This is like saying that a baby normally must crawl before he can walk. In the same way it might be said that it is important for a young man to learn how to be a good husband before he takes on the additional responsibilities of being a good father.

THROUGH THE ELEMENT OF REINFORCEMENT

This principle suggests that learning is greatly facilitated through achievement, recognition for good performance, and the encouragement of the teacher in general. The effective teacher, therefore, wisely uses recognition and appreciation to stimulate his students toward further effort.

THROUGH EMPHASIS ON COMPREHENSION

Perhaps the most important aspect of the entire learning process is the matter of comprehension. The Christian teacher is always concerned that the children, young people, or adults whom he is teaching genuinely understand the meaning of the truth of God. Memorization of Scripture and recitation of facts can be helpful in the learning process, but ultimately Christian teaching is concerned with thoughtful application of these verses and facts.

NOTES

1. John Milton Gregory, *The Seven Laws of Teaching* (Grand Rapids: Baker Book House, 1954), p.5.
2. Ernest M. Ligon, *A Greater Generation* (New York: Macmillan Co., 1948).
3. Op. cit., p.5.

STUDY PROJECTS

1. Write your own definition of learning.
2. List five Christian doctrines and indicate sensory experiences which can be used to teach them to children.
3. In what ways can a teacher make his teaching content more interesting?

4. Define several ways in which satisfactory class work can be reinforced.
5. Give three examples of teaching methods that recognize the learning characteristics of young people.

BIBLIOGRAPHY

Brubaker, J. Omar, and Clark, Robert E. **Understanding People.** Wheaton, IL: Evangelical Teacher Training Association, 1981.

Edge, Findley B. **Teaching for Results.** Nashville: Broadman Press, 1956.

Horne, Herman H. **Teaching Techniques of Jesus.** Rev. ed. Grand Rapids: Kregel Publications, 1971. Chapters 19-21.

Richards, Lawrence O. **Creative Bible Teaching.** Chicago: Moody Press, 1970. Part I, pp. 5-63.

Sound Principles
of
Teaching

What is the value of objectives in Christian teaching?
How important is motivation in teaching?
What is meant by life-relatedness?
How is the Bible used in problem solving?

Underneath good teaching are basic guidelines for the whole teaching process; the teacher understands something about what good teaching is and how it goes on; he recognizes the elements of the learning process and how he as a teacher must deal with them in order to engage in effective communication.

From this follows the selection of the means for this communication. The teacher must determine the methodology necessary to get the message across. Finally, the teacher is concerned with supplementing his method through the use of good teaching aids.

The order of this teaching preparation is important. This chapter considers the underlying principles of teaching. Later chapters will consider the subjects of methods and aids.

THE PRINCIPLE OF OBJECTIVE

It has been said that we have a much better chance of hitting the target if we can see it.

A statement of objective is a definition by the teacher of what he expects to accomplish in the teaching process. Clear objectives are essential to any teaching-learning effort. The statement of a goal may not guarantee its achievement, but it is a necessary first step in that direction. It will be noted that the words "objective," "goal," and "aim" are used interchangeably in this chapter.

CHARACTERISTICS OF GOOD OBJECTIVES

There are certain marks which characterize a good objective. Findley Edge has suggested that the statement of objective should be *brief* enough to be remembered, *clear* enough to be written down, and *specific* enough to be achieved. [1] Such general statements as "I want to be a blessing to my class," or "I hope to teach the lesson adequately," are too ambiguous to be evaluated properly or of value as objectives.

The good objective also will be *flexible* enough to allow for changes in the teaching situation. For example, you might anticipate that all of the students coming to your class on a given Sunday will be Christians, and therefore you plan without particular emphasis on evangelism. But when you arrive at the class you find that one of your students has brought an unsaved friend. You will, then, want to allow sufficient flexibility within your lesson objectives to clearly present the gospel somewhere in that class period.

Also, good lesson objectives ought to be in terms of *student behavior*. The real measure of teaching success is what happens in the lives of the students—not how polished the performance of the teacher in the classroom may have been. Try to think in terms of what happens to your students when you teach, and keep them central in the objectives.

EXAMPLES OF OBJECTIVES

What are some worthy general objectives for Christian teaching? Certainly *evangelism* would be primary. We teach so that others may learn the truth of the gospel and put their trust in the

Savior. *Christian commitment* is another worthy objective. Paul clearly calls for the Christian to surrender his life to Christ (Romans 12:1,2), and the Christian teacher is a vehicle of this divine message to his students.

Beyond these general objectives there are also the more detailed goals of individual lessons or series of lessons. For example, a teacher of primary boys may select as his objective for a given quarter the *teaching of genuine obedience*. A high school teacher may want his young people to seriously consider *God's call to vocational Christian service*. A teacher of preschool children may aim to teach his children *how to express a public prayer*.

TYPES OF OBJECTIVES
Relating To Content And Behavior
Some aims have to do with factual content; others with action. Both have a place in Christian teaching, for it is important both to know the Bible and to apply it in Christian living. The teacher needs to be aware of the difference and keep his lesson aims clearly defined.

Relating To Year, Quarter, And Week
The Christian teacher will want to establish at the beginning of the teaching *year* some of the things that he hopes to see accomplished in the lives of his students throughout that year. Then, as he receives the Sunday school material for each new *quarter*, he will develop more specific objectives related to the lesson content for that quarter. Finally, in the preparation of each *week*, the teacher will be very specific about what should be accomplished through his teaching ministry on a given Sunday. The general principle here is that the more immediate the teaching situation, the more detailed will become the objectives.

Relating To Individual, Church, And Home
An adequate treatment of objectives will touch on a variety of relationships. Thus, students will need to see the truth related to them as *individuals* in the matter of salvation or recognizing God's call in their lives. In a broader perspective they will need to see how the individual relates to the *church* in its ministries both locally and around the world. There also needs to be emphasis on the individual's relationship to the *home*. If you are teaching children, the matters of obedience and love in the home are primary. If you are teaching parents, the goals of submission, love, and family care become vital.

23

THE PRINCIPLE OF INVOLVEMENT

In the days when workers learned a vocation through apprenticeship training, much opportunity was provided for practical experience in the trade. This presents an important principle of the teaching-learning process: learning through participation.

The effective teacher will provide many opportunities for group and individual participation and involvement. Chapters five and six describe various ways for involving class members. A teacher employing this approach to teaching would include learning activities and projects, discussion, and many creative opportunities for interaction and involvement. Since the class members are actively involved in learning, many refer to this concept as "discovery learning." Teachers determine the objectives and then select techniques which allow class members to get directly involved in accomplishing these objectives.

THE IMPORTANCE OF INVOLVEMENT

Educators today agree on the importance of drawing the student into his own learning process. The matter of involvement is important in teaching children, essential in teaching young people, and imperative in teaching adults. Involvement recognizes the fact that in the teaching process there must be a two-way communication between the teacher and the student. A number of ways in which this can be accomplished will be discussed in the section on methods. When a teacher applies the principle of involvement, he selects teaching methods which develop this principle.

THE MOTIVATION OF INVOLVEMENT

Any discussion of the development of involvement leads immediately into the matter of motivation. One of the biggest problems that is faced by all education, Christian and secular, is this problem of getting the student to actively desire the learning which he needs. The Christian teacher has more difficulty with this than the public school teacher for the latter has access to external motivation in the form of grades, graduation, and required attendance. Though the creation of motivation may be difficult, it is essential to the learning process.

THE RESULTS OF INVOLVEMENT

When the student comes to the place where he recognizes the importance of what he is learning, and desires to put it into practice in his life day by day, the work of the teacher has been greatly helped. Such involvement will lead to a practice of the truth which is the ultimate concern of the Christian teacher. It also causes the student to study and prepare outside of class, greatly enhancing the value of the class period.

THE PRINCIPLE OF RELEVANCY

Relevancy simply means that the ideas which are given to people must be related to the situations in which they find themselves at the time they hear those ideas. This is life-relatedness. The teacher can only be sure of his success in communicating truth when he sees that truth operative in the lives of his students. The teacher who is content with a rote memorization of unapplied facts has missed the purpose and process of real teaching.

LIFE-RELATEDNESS IS A KEY TO INTEREST

Any student will learn better if he is interested in that which he is studying. We know from recent surveys of teenagers who have dropped out of church that one of the precipitating causes was their failure to see any connection between what the church taught and their everyday lives. Therefore, they lost interest in what the church was teaching and in the church itself.

LIFE-RELATEDNESS IS A KEY TO INVOLVEMENT

The good teacher develops in his students a spirit of relevant inquiry which will lead them into self-directed study. Such a teacher is never satisfied with mere transmission of knowledge, but continues to stimulate and spark the student until there arises from the spark a small fire of understanding and involvement which can burn its way to real learning.

LIFE-RELATEDNESS IS A KEY TO APPLICATION

Consider our Lord's words in Matthew 7:20-24 where he clearly emphasizes the importance of life application of Christian teaching:

> Wherefore by their fruits ye shall know them. Not every one that saith unto me, Lord, Lord, shall enter into the kingdom of heaven; but he that doeth the will of my Father which is in heaven. Many will say to me in that day, Lord, Lord, have we not prophesied in thy name? and in thy name have cast out devils? and in thy name done many wonderful works? And then will I profess unto them, I never knew you: depart from me, ye that work iniquity. Therefore whosoever heareth these sayings of mine, and doeth them, I will liken him unto a wise man, which built his house upon a rock.

The teacher should never take for granted that a student understands and knows how to apply the principles of the Bible to his life. The teaching of such understanding and application is the responsibility of the teacher and assumes, of course, that the teacher has first learned to apply Scripture in his own life.

LIFE-RELATEDNESS IS A KEY TO CHRISTIAN GROWTH

Spiritual life change, whether regeneration or sanctification, is the work of the Spirit of God and not of any man. The responsibility of the teacher, however, is to relate God's truth so carefully to the life of the student that the Spirit of God can then make that truth a daily living experience.

THE PRINCIPLE OF PROBLEM-SOLVING

One of the great lacks in churches today is that many of God's people do not know how to use the Word of God themselves. Often teachers have not taught their students how to be dependent upon the Holy Spirit and to feed themselves spiritually from the Scriptures.

TEACH THE STUDENT TO SEARCH FOR HIMSELF

A teacher's work is involved with making the student an independent investigator of the subject. The purpose is not to solve the problems for the student, but to teach him how to deal with his own problems from the Word of God. The fact that we are dealing with God's truths does not mean that we are forced into transmissive methods of communicating that truth. Truth will mean much more to the student when he is led to discover it for himself, rather than simply being informed by a teacher.

TEACH THE STUDENT TO SOLVE HIS OWN PROBLEMS

In a sense, the Christian teacher is as much a communicator of techniques as of content. If all the student knows when he leaves the class is the amount of knowledge the teacher has been able to transmit from his mind to the student, the time which was spent together has not been used to the greatest profit. When the student runs out of the transmitted knowledge, or encounters a problem which somehow does not seem to fit into the framework of that information, his only recourse will be to turn back to the teacher or to someone else, to find the answers. The teacher must be concerned not only with teaching the student what he himself has learned, but also how he has learned it.

TEACH THE STUDENT TO TEACH OTHERS

The process of problem-solving should initiate in a student the principles of leadership and Christian maturity which will enable him not only to help himself, but also to help others in their Christian growth. This is well presented in the words of Paul to young Timothy: "And the things that thou hast heard of me among many witnesses, the same commit thou to faithful men, who shall be able to teach others also" (II Tim. 2:2).

The development of sound principles of teaching stands at the beginning of the teaching-learning process. If we fail here, we are greatly weakened in our selection of methods, gathering of materials, and actual execution of the teaching process. On the other hand, the recognition and practice of these principles provide a good basis for effective communication.

NOTES

1. Findley B. Edge, *Teaching for Results* (Nashville: Broadman Press, 1956).

STUDY PROJECTS

1. Using either a class that you are presently teaching or a clearly defined teaching situation, write a set of objectives for a year of teaching.
2. Based on the same situation as in question one, describe specific behavorial changes that you wish to see in your students during the next six months.
3. Name some specific ways students can be engaged in involvement in the teaching process.
4. Write a one sentence definition in your own words of each of the four major principles discussed in this chapter.

BIBLIOGRAPHY

Edge, Findley B. **Teaching for Results.** Nashville: Broadman Press, 1956.

Richards, Lawrence O. **Creative Bible Teaching.** Chicago: Moody Press, 1970. Part II, pp. 67-143.

Uys, Sue. **Successful Bible Teaching.** Grand Rapids: Baker Book House, 1973.

Zuck, Roy B. **Spiritual Power in Your Teaching.** Rev. ed. Chicago: Moody Press, 1972.

Introduction
to
Teaching Methods

What types of teaching methods are available for the Christian teacher?
How does the teacher develop variety in his teaching?
What factors contribute to student involvement?
How does one choose a proper teaching method?

Effective teaching calls for understanding the best teaching methods for specific learning situations.

Because age groups differ in such areas as interest, mental ability, and attention span, the teacher must choose teaching methods that are appropriate for his group. Children, for example, have learning characteristics that differ considerably from those of adults, and teaching methods which may be very effective with adults will not necessarily achieve communication with children.

Choice of teaching method is indeed a crucial part of the teaching process. This chapter and the two which follow concentrate on the understanding and proper selection of methods.

CATEGORIES OF METHODS

The variety of teaching methods is almost limitless. It may be helpful, therefore, to think of categories of methods and place specific methods within the following general categories.

TEACHER TO STUDENT COMMUNICATION

This is an emphasis on the teacher as the performer in the educational process. Such methodology as lecture, story telling, and demonstration would be placed here.

STUDENT TO TEACHER COMMUNICATION

In this category the student is the major performer, with the teacher basically in a listening roll. Such methods as recitation, reports, and testing would be included.

TEACHER WITH STUDENT COMMUNICATION

This, in the opinion of a large portion of professional educators, is the best approach for the teaching-learning process. It is an approach which involves teacher and student in a mutual quest for truth. Two familiar examples of this type of method are class discussion and question and answer.

GROUP ACTIVITY

There is a wide range of group activity that can be utilized as teaching method, and this approach is finding increasing development and use in education. Activities as panels, debates, discussion groups, buzz groups, and all forms of drama could be categorized under this general heading.

INSTRUCTIVE PLAY

This category of teaching method is usually used with children from cradle roll to junior age. Examples in this classification include educational games and toys, sand table, puppets, finger plays, puzzles, simple role playing, and action songs.

NON-CLASSROOM ACTIVITY

In a serious educational program the teacher is concerned that the student prepare himself for a class by studying in advance. Guided preparation carefully related to subsequent class sessions can contribute much to spiritual growth. This category actually extends itself beyond preparation and includes such things as field trips, research, and projects.

VARIETY IN TEACHING METHOD

An old adage states that "variety is the spice of life" and this certainly has an application to the classroom. Two questions will help us consider this subject from the aspect of teaching methods.

DEVELOPING VARIETY

Become Acquainted With Various Methods

The teacher cannot use a method with which he is unfamiliar. It is important, therefore, to become acquainted with as many methods as practical. This text provides one opportunity for this.

Use Lesson Plans For Analysis

Variety of methods implies an understanding of what has been done in the past. Records must be available, and one procedure for gaining an analysis of methodology is to use one's lesson plan sheets. Lesson plan sheets are described in a later section of the book.

Constantly Evaluate Yourself As A Teacher

The teacher's own attitude toward his ministry is very important. He must consider his teaching to be service for Christ, which must meet high standards. Variety in methodology is one facet of the excellence which should be his goal.

USING DIFFERENT METHODS

There are two common expressions which often deter advancement in teaching or administration. One states about a new teaching idea: "It won't work." The other is similar: "It may be good but it won't work here." Effective answers to such attitudes require thorough knowledge of the new method and recognition that some methods may have to be in effect for a period of time before their value can be finally judged.

New methods may be learned:

By Reading Books On Teaching

This text is a basic introduction to teaching. The books listed in the bibliography at the end of each chapter provide the earnest teacher with resources for further study.

By Watching Good Teachers In Action

Ministry can be enhanced by taking time to observe other

teachers in their own classroom settings. If possible, observers should watch teachers who are teaching approximately the same age level and general content. Notes should be made during observation and discussed with the teacher afterwards. Points of procedure that were new or about which questions were raised should also be discussed. It is usual courtesy to make an appointment for observation before visitation.

By Experience
Teachers are sometimes discouraged with results the first few times they use a new method. However, continued effort and experience are a necessary part of worthwhile progress.

THE PLACE OF INVOLVEMENT
IMPORTANCE OF INVOLVEMENT
Among the teaching principles discussed in chapter 3, the principle of involvement has special significance for teaching methods. As was implied in that chapter, involvement, or participation, is not an option; it is a necessity in the adequate learning situation. Since involvement is largely determined by methods, it follows that an appreciation of involvement's importance directly influences the teacher's choice of method.

FACTORS IN INVOLVEMENT
Room arrangement and equipment are important considerations in effective involvement procedures. Proper size chairs and suitable tables contribute to involvement. If the room is large enough and chairs are mobile, consider a semi-circle or even a complete circle. Rather than standing by a lecturn, the teacher might also sit in the circle. Sitting with children around a small table is usually an aid in securing their participation. Generally, the room should have the appearance of a group workshop rather than a lecture hall.

Questions are a key factor in participation methodology. Those which have a yes or no answer, or simple factual information answer, rarely lead to group participation. Proper questions are discussed in a later chapter.

Finally, it should be noted that participation doesn't just happen. It is carefully pre-planned by the teacher. Each of the methods that relate to involvement requires a significant amount of preparation on the part of the teacher to become effective.

FACTORS IN CHOOSING A METHOD

Selection of a proper teaching method takes into consideration certain key factors. Like many other habits of good teaching, this becomes a mental process which the experienced teacher does almost automatically in effective lesson preparation.

OBJECTIVES OF THE LESSON

This is a foundational consideration in the choice of method. What goals are to be accomplished in the classroom period? Can the goals chosen be achieved best through a large amount of student participation or do they require the teacher to present considerable content? The teacher's clear understanding of his lesson goals will help determine how he goes about accomplishing them.

AGE GROUP OF THE STUDENTS

As already noted, the age of the students affects their responses to different methods. It would be impractical to use adult lecture method to teach primaries. On the other hand, the use of a simple Bible story would usually be insufficient for adult study. The teacher must consider the age of his students before selecting a teaching method.

CONTENT OF THE LESSON

A historical lesson from the book of Acts for high schoolers could lend itself well to an illustrated presentation with the use of good Bible maps. On the other hand, the principles of Christian separation expounded by the Apostle Paul in the sixth chapter of I Corinthians would be handled better in that group through open discussion.

AVAILABLE RESOURCES

Small group work for a class requires sufficient room space. It would be useless to plan for a filmstrip if no projector were available for the teacher's use. It is important to know about and check on availability of all the materials and equipment needed for the method being considered.

EDUCATIONAL BACKGROUND OF THE STUDENTS

Age, as we have already noted, is not the only factor in determining maturity. Just as important, is the student's background knowledge. A class of young adults, most of whom were new Christians, would have difficulty participating in any deep discussion of some of the principles of Bible prophecy. The student's spiritual maturity helps guide method, as well as content.

ALLOTTED TIME

Some teaching methods require much more time for effective use than others. Careful provision must be made for proper timing. If buzz groups are used, for example, sufficient time should be allowed to hear the reports from the various groups and tie the whole discussion together with some concluding remarks.

STUDY PROJECTS

1. Illustrate from your own experience or observation the difference between teacher to student and teacher with student methods of teaching.
2. Prepare a sample lesson showing how discussion would be used differently with children, youth, and adult classes.
3. Make a comprehensive list of the teaching methods that would be appropriate for an age group of your selection.
4. Teach a class, including a teaching method you have not used before.
5. Make arrangements to observe an experienced teacher in the age group in which you are interested.

BIBLIOGRAPHY

Bingham, Robert E. **New Ways of Teaching the Old Story.** Nashville: Broadman Press, 1970.

Edge, Findley B. **Helping the Teacher.** Nashville: Broadman Press, 1959. Chapter 9.

Gangel, Kenneth O. **24 Ways to Improve Your Teaching.** Wheaton, IL: Victor Books, 1974. Pages 7-11.

Let's Talk About Teaching. Wheaton, IL: Evangelical Teacher Training Association, 1969.

Leypoldt, Martha M. **40 Ways to Teach in Groups.** Valley Forge, PA: Judson Press, 1967. Pages 15-36.

Teaching Methods
That Focus On
Teacher Or Group

What is the place of the lecture method in teaching?
In what sense is testing a teaching method?
What are the values of group projects?
How can role playing be used as a teaching method?

This chapter discusses two major categories of method. The first section of the chapter presents methods that focus on the *teacher*, either as a performer or as a receiver of student response. The methods presented are lecture, storytelling, memorization and recitation, and testing.

The second section emphasizes *group* methods. Projects, instructive play, role playing, and group activity are presented as illustrations in this category.

To help the reader evaluate the methods, each one is discussed briefly in terms of its values, its difficulties, and suggestions for its use.

METHODS THAT FOCUS ON THE TEACHER

LECTURE

In the lecture method the teacher presents the lesson largely by speaking directly to the class.

Values

The lecture method of teaching makes possible the covering of considerable material in minimum time. It lends itself to work in large groups. With the teacher determining the material to be presented, class time can be kept centered on the subject at hand. Minimum class preparation is necessary for the students.

Difficulties

The lecture method can become boring unless the teacher keeps the presentation fresh and meaningful for his listeners. With class participation usually limited, student creativity and initiative can be stifled as the teacher remains the only performer in the classroom.

Further difficulties in this method are that it does not allow the teacher to observe the reactions of the students; there is little provision for individual difference of students; and questions may go unanswered throughout the entire class period.

Suggestions For Use

1. Combine lecture with other methods of teaching which provide class involvement.

2. Use visuals where possible to clarify the content of the lecture.

3. Have very clear objectives and teaching outlines.

STORYTELLING

This is a basic form of teaching used with small children. Stories of all types and for every situation are available for providing basic knowledge throughout childhood. An occasional story well told to youth or adults may also serve educational purposes.

Values

Storytelling has an important principle of learning built into it—interest. Often that which children cannot or will not learn by direct instruction can be taught to them through a story.

Difficulties

A preliminary difficulty is often an unwillingness to try the method. Other difficulties are the tendency to read the story rather than tell it or make the story too long.

Suggestions For Use

1. Prepare thoroughly enough to tell the story without reading.
2. Use stories that will have meaning for the listener.
3. Use words which describe sensory experience, such as "fuzzy" and "shiny."
4. Avoid making the story so long that it loses interest.

MEMORIZATION AND RECITATION

Values

In the use of teaching methods which utilize student to teacher communication processes, the teacher gains an understanding of the student's level of knowledge and achievement through being a listener. Also, the student becomes actively involved in the learning process.

Difficulties

There still exists in this method the limitation of one-way communication, even though the speaking role has been shifted from teacher to student. Furthermore, there is need to carefully guard against rote memory without understanding.

Suggestions For Use

The value of recitation and memorization as a teaching method can be enhanced if the following guidelines are applied:

1. Seek to make all material to be memorized meaningful to the student.
2. Apply review principles to strengthen learning retention.
3. When a memorization assignment has been made, give the student opportunity to demonstrate that he has achieved.
4. Utilize available visual materials to increase the memorization potential of the student.

TESTING

Testing has often been viewed as a measurement or disciplinary device. However, when rightly understood and used, testing can also be classified as a teaching method.

Values

Testing gives the teacher some idea of the student's comprehension level. There is also a motivation here which may at first be purely external, but which can lead to self-discipline and self-motivated learning.

Difficulties

Testing takes the teacher's time for test preparation, administering the test to the class, and grading. In a church situation testing may initially set up a negative reaction on the part of the students, and this dislike for tests must be overcome by demonstrating their value.

Suggestions For Use

1. Relate each question to some particular learning experience and avoid emphasis on mere factual memorization.

2. Give the student opportunity to prepare by announcing tests well in advance. Clearly define the purpose of the test.

3. Grade and return tests as soon as possible to retain learning value. Use tests as opportunity for review.

4. Avoid placing too much emphasis on the results of any one test. Student's backgrounds, physical condition, and related factors must be considered in evaluating test results.

METHODS THAT EMPHASIZE GROUP WORK
GROUP PROJECTS

Projects can be carried on by a teacher and class either during the classroom period or as an outside activity. Project ideas include observation and report, writing (such as a junior high class rewriting a chapter of the Bible in contemporary language), construction (such as a model tabernacle), or service projects (such as gospel team work or institutional visitation). All of these ideas emphasize the group doing something together under guidance.

Values

The use of projects can greatly increase the value of class time, particularly when the project is carried on outside of class. A group of young people studying a unit in personal evangelism, for example, might add significantly to their learning through a missions ministry or tract distribution project. A good project methodology often ties the lesson and the classroom to the real life activities of the student.

Difficulties

A great deal of flexibility is required on the part of the teacher. He cannot be a mere transmitter of information, but must become a guide and motivator. Expense for project materials must also be considered.

Suggestions For Use

A few simple guidelines will help the teacher keep the method effective.

1. Make sure that the project is specifically related in content and objective to the lesson being studied.

2. Evaluate the project carefully for degree of difficulty to avoid having students become discouraged by a project that is beyond their ability to handle.

3. Do not let the project go so long that the students begin to lose interest. It sometimes helps to break a larger project into stages of development that permit satisfaction for the completion of each stage.

INSTRUCTIVE PLAY

Instructive play is play directed toward learning experiences. This type of methodology is most effective in the preschool and primary years.

Values

The principle of interest discussed earlier explains why so many preschool and kindergarten programs are built on instructive play. The teacher develops a favorable attitude on the part of the child because the child is having fun while he is learning. This facilitates securing attention as well as understanding of the content.

Difficulties

No doubt the major difficulty here is allowing instructive play to degenerate into just play without educational objectives. There also needs to be an alertness to the possibility of discipline problems. The teacher must be in control of the classroom at all times.

Suggestions For Use

1. Seek to gain a good understanding of the educational use

of play activities before using this method.

2. Keep play activities under control by having adequate staff.

3. Plan the class session so that a time of exuberant play does not immediately precede a worship time.

4. Make certain that noise or commotion resulting from using instructive play does not disturb other classes.

ROLE PLAYING

In role playing the student seeks to understand and act out a particular part of another person's life.

Values

Role playing produces empathy which is a helpful ingredient in the learning process. The student must think in terms of the person being studied. Hopefully, the student will gain added understanding of himself, and the class will recognize problems and solutions to those problems through the role. Role playing is also stimulus for discussion.

Difficulties

Sometimes it is difficult to motivate students to participate in role playing. They may feel embarrassed and wish not to get involved. Occasionally, the acting out of a role may become humorous, and the serious emphasis becomes lost.

Suggestions For Use

1. Clearly define the role to be played and explain its relationship to the lesson.

2. Select participants, but do not force anyone into a role which he does not wish to play.

GROUP ACTIVITY

The activities in this category depend especially on the interaction or dynamics of a group situation. Activities such as panels, debates, discussion groups, and buzz groups are listed under this general heading.

Values

This method encourages the development of the students as they are drawn into participation and activity. It involves a maximum number of students in the learning process at any given time.

Difficulties

Group process is not simply an unstructured classroom situation. On the contrary, it requires thorough preparation, and it is often far more difficult for a teacher to assure a *properly functioning* group process than to deliver a lecture in the classroom.

Suggestions For Use

1. Before using any group process, have clearly in mind just what results are expected and how the particular activity to be used will accomplish them. Do not take results for granted.

2. Do not force shy students to take part in large group activity. Instead, arrange for small groups that will encourage natural participation.

3. Give clear preparation assignments that will help students prepare for intelligent participation in the group activity.

An observation of the teaching methods used by our Lord revealed many of the things which are being mentioned in these chapters. There was always in his ministry an inseparability between methodology and the principle of life-relatedness in teaching. The purpose of the methodology was always to secure the distinct translation of truth to life. Perhaps our teaching will result more in changed lives if greater attention is given to the way in which we attempt to communicate truth.

STUDY PROJECTS

1. Suggest changes you might make in a lesson using either lecture or storytelling (one you have taught or heard taught recently), if you were to teach it next week.
2. Find a common object around your house or yard and develop a ten-minute lesson about the object which illustrates some biblical truth.
3. Prepare a fifteen-question test on the book of Ruth geared to a specific age group, with each question aimed at emphasizing a particular truth in the study.
4. Select a Bible story (one that relates to your current lessons if you are presently teaching) and prepare a written study on how it could be adapted for role playing with a class.
5. Write a lesson plan utilizing the project method.

BIBLIOGRAPHY

Barrett, Ethel. **Storytelling, It's Easy!** Grand Rapids: Zondervan Pub. House, 1960.

Edge, Findley B. **Helping the Teacher.** Nashville: Broadman Press, 1959. Chapters 10, 11.

Ford, LeRoy. **Using the Lecture in Teaching and Training.** Nashville: Broadman Press, 1968.

Gangel, Kenneth O. **24 Ways to Improve Your Teaching.** Wheaton, IL: Victor Books, 1974. Chapters 1-4, 12-18, 22-24.

Teaching Methods
That Focus On
Teacher-Student Cooperation

What problems exist in teaching adults?
How is preclass preparation secured?
What methods provide for mutual quest for truth?
How can a teacher encourage his class to participate in discussion?

It is the opinion of many educators that the best approach to the teaching-learning process is through a method that involves teacher and student in a mutual quest for truth. Since both parties in such a process are constantly relating to each other, this type of methodology might be designated "dual communication."

RELATIONSHIP TO ADULTS

Methods emphasizing teacher-student cooperation are applicable in work with junior high age and above. They become especially pertinent in the college and adult years, where teachers face specific adult problems in communication. There is often a lack of interest on the part of the students; sometimes faulty early education stands in the way of satisfactory learning; and many times adults fail to understand or be concerned with their own needs. To meet these problems, the teacher of adults must not only teach, but as part of his teaching seek to develop in the adult a genuine involvement in his own learning process.

An essential preliminary to adult work is the recognition that adults can learn. Actually, learning ability never wears out. The Adult Education Association notes that "Age as age probably does little to affect an individual's power to learn or to think."[1] It may take additional effort on the part of adults to learn satisfactorily, but if the effort is put forth, absorption and retention will take place.

RELATIONSHIP TO PRECLASS PREPARATION

If the student is to participate intelligently in the learning process, there must be preparation on his part. He must have basic knowledge of the subject in order to participate meaningfully. While the principles suggested here have specific application for methods emphasizing a mutual quest for learning, they also apply to teaching methods in general.

THE BENEFITS OF PRECLASS PREPARATION

It Raises The Educational Level Of A Class

Home study adds greatly to the educational value of a class. Achievement increases and the value of class time is enhanced for those who have been motivated to prepare in advance.

It Increases The Learning Period

Learning is normally a process not a single event. Certainly there are moments when an idea really takes hold. However, it requires a period of time for the student to comprehend and apply information sufficiently to state that it has been learned. Work on the lesson material during the week extends the educational time factor far beyond the limits of the classroom hour.

It Helps Relate Study To Life And The School To The Home

All of life ought to be a learning process and all of Christian truth should relate to life. As the student brings his study into the home it broadens the learning process from a classroom situation to a wider application. It should become natural for him to study and apply to his life the Bible and lessons outside as well as in the classroom.

It Stimulates A Spirit Of Inquiry

The process of home study often produces questions and reactions that can be profitably brought into the classroom. This provides stimulus and material for discussion and classroom involvement.

TYPES OF PRECLASS PREPARATION

Lesson Material Assignments

Sometimes the published curriculum materials which the teacher is using provide for various kinds of study assignments. The teacher must evaluate these in terms of his class situation. All assignments should be given in a way that provides interest and motivation.

Reading And Research

Reading assignments can be given for the Bible or for other supplementary helps. Research can be assigned in terms of Bible dictionaries, Bible encyclopedias, commentaries, or other resource materials.

Interviews

This might be classed as a special area of research. A group studying a missionary series, for example, could be encouraged to interview by telephone or in person missionaries who are in the area.

An important point in preclass preparation is that the teacher recognize work which the students have done. Students will soon become disinterested if assignments are made but not referred to again, or used in any way.

METHODS THAT ILLUSTRATE TEACHER-STUDENT COOPERATION

The emphasis in these methods of teaching is on verbal exchange between two persons. Primarily this exchange, or dialogue, takes place between the teacher and a student, although it may also be between students under the guidance of a teacher or leader.

DISCUSSION

A good discussion is a cooperative search for truth. It differs from the question and answer method both in the kind of questions which are asked (e.g., explanation rather than simple information), and also in the fact that discussion is not limited to a question approach.

Values

A discussion awakens interest in the subject and guides the thinking of the students. It allows participation for the student in terms of sharing his ideas as well as raising his questions. In the process the teacher gains an insight into student progress and the class member is taught expression technique as well as basic content.

Difficulties

A discussion may require the teacher to think spontaneously, and it also involves a good background on the subject being considered. A discussion further needs time for a group to work through a problem. Even so, the conclusion may be incorrect even though the majority of the students agree with it. Sometimes there is a tendency to divert from the subject.

Suggestions For Use

1. A good discussion builds on questions and interchange of ideas. Guide a discussion with these so that it leads to continuing interest and topic development.

2. To encourage maximum participation, strive for an atmosphere of freedom and flexibility so that all sides of an issue can be covered.

3. Be careful that reaction to a student's contribution does not squelch initiative and inhibit further participation.

4. At the end of a discussion make certain that some conclusions are formed or direction established.

QUESTION AND ANSWER

Questions raise curiosity and interest and are stimuli for learning. A carefully worded question by a capable teacher can assist the student both to review learnings and to increase knowledge as he searches for answers still unknown.

Values

The question and answer method enables the teacher to focus on a particular lesson point and obtain class interest on that point. It can be used in conjunction with almost every other teaching method. Because of its adaptability, this method can also be used with almost any age group.

Difficulties

A major difficulty in using question and answer methodology lies in the choosing of appropriate questions. It is not difficult to ask a question, but it requires considerable thought to ask those that will give maximum help to individual students as well as maximum focus on the lesson point. There is also the problem of embarrassing students by asking questions for which they are unprepared.

Suggestions For Use

1. Plan your questions in advance to clearly relate to the point at which they are asked.

2. Avoid monopoly of the question and answer time by any one student.

3. Once again, avoid purely negative teacher reaction to students' answers. In an answer that is foolish or erroneous, try to find opportunity for positive teaching and helpful guidance.

RESEARCH AND REPORTS

Research and reports become most productive when the student works with his teacher on an individual basis. Guided by good counsel in his study, the student also can contribute to the enrichment of his peers by a well presented report of his discoveries.

Values

As a student and a teacher work together in developing a research report, a kind of informal interchange takes place which is a valuable educational process. Written research followed by public reporting is also a key means for increased meaning and retention.

Difficulties

Time and resources are problems to be considered here. Unless the church library is well stocked or the student has access to a private library such as that owned by the pastor, extensive research in Bible-related areas may be quite difficult. Time is a factor for both teacher and student as they are involved in the research.

Suggestions For Use

1. Provide sufficient resource guidance for the student to do an adequate job. Supply or direct to a source for such materials as will be needed.

2. Use research projects that are practical and have interest appeal to the students.

3. Encouragement and follow-up is often necessary after the initial assignment has been given in order to insure fulfillment.

DEBATES AND PANELS

Debates and panels have their basic emphasis on interchange of ideas. A debate is a highly structured presentation of two sides of a statement, whereas a panel is a grouping of several people for a somewhat structured discussion on a given subject.

Values

Debates and panels get the student very actively involved in the learning process. He can no longer be a passive recipient of information. He himself must initiate and respond to information. This calls for preparation. Also, debates and panels usually develop considerable interest on the part of the entire class.

Difficulties

A major concern with these methods is adequate preparation on the part of the debaters or panelists. There is also the risk of having an important member of the group not appear at the time of presentation.

Suggestions For Use

1. Plan panels and debates sufficiently in advance to permit adequate preparation.

2. Questions and issues assigned for debate must be clearcut and have definite pros and cons.

CREATIVE WRITING

In creative writing the student may work with the teacher to develop a creditable piece of written material. It may range from Christian poetry to Christian drama and from a simple testimony to a thorough doctrinal study.

Values

Creative writing can provide the teacher with information about the student's progress and ability at a given point. It allows the student to draw upon his inner resources to put his feelings and thoughts in written form.

Difficulties

The same two major difficulties of time and resources which were noted with reference to debates and panels exist also in the area of creative writing.

Suggestions For Use

1. Creative writing can be utilized for both in-class and out-of-class work.

2. Both during the writing and on its completion, the work should form the basis for profitable discussion between the teacher and the student.

3. Allow as much student freedom in the selection of subjects and problems for writing as the class objectives will permit.

Teacher-student cooperative effort provides the teacher with constant opportunity to ascertain what the student has learned and where he stands in the teaching-learning process. The user of these methods will find it helpful, therefore, to ask himself the following evaluation questions:

1. Did the members of the class secure information through this method which they would not have gained otherwise?

2. Was their thinking clarified through use of this method?

3. Have they been able to come to more meaningful conclusions because they have been allowed to participate in the learning process?

NOTES

1. Irving Lorge, *et al., Psychology of Adults,* Washington, D.C.: Adult Education Association of the U.S.A., 1963, p.4.

STUDY PROJECTS

1. State all the reasons you think of which makes it difficult to involve a class in discussion. Study each of the items you have listed and suggest several possibilities for solving the problem, using the material in this chapter where possible.

2. Study carefully I Corinthians 13. Write from it five factual questions which might be used for question and answer, and five thought-provoking questions which could be used in a discussion.
3. Look over a month's lesson series and list which subjects would lend themselves to research and reports.
4. From the same lesson series, write down five topics which would be effective for creative writing projects.

BIBLIOGRAPHY

Edge, Findley B. **Helping the Teacher.** Nashville: Broadman Press, 1959. Chapters 6, 7.

Ford, LeRoy. **Using the Panel in Teaching and Training.** Nashville: Broadman Press, 1970.

Gangel, Kenneth O. **24 Ways to Improve Your Teaching.** Wheaton, IL: Victor Books, 1974. Chapters 5-11, 19-21.

LeFever, Marlene D. **Turnabout Teaching.** Elgin, IL: D.C. Cook Pub. Co., 1973.

Leypoldt, Martha M. **40 Ways to Teach in Groups.** Valley Forge, PA: Judson Press, 1967.

Instructional Aids

And

Teaching

What is an instructional aid?
What is the relationship of instructional aids to teaching principles and
 methods?
What types of instructional aids can be used in teaching?
What are proper guidelines for determining when and how to use instruc-
 tional aids?

Instructional aids are physical tools which facilitate communication through appeal to sensory perception. If we show the student something or let him hear or do something, he will be more
likely to achieve understanding than if we just talk to him about it.

Various figures have been given for the percentage of retention
accomplished by using methods emphasizing hearing, seeing, or
doing. Regardless of percentages major research on the subject
indicates that the teacher who uses as many of the sensory gates as
possible will be most likely to communicate effectively to his
students.

Good teaching is done by the teacher who first of all understands the proper principles of good teaching, then selects correct methods for communication, and finally supports his teaching with adequate instructional aids.

TYPES OF INSTRUCTIONAL AIDS

There are many different kinds of teaching aids. Some are audio, some are visual, and some are both audio and visual.

AUDIO MATERIALS

This category includes radio, tape recordings, and phonograph records. Tape recordings and phonograph records are used for such activites as teaching gospel songs, listening to stories told by an expert, and in connection with visual presentations.

NON-PROJECTED STILL PICTURES

In this category are such items as drawings, flat pictures, flash cards, photographs, posters, and murals. Most Sunday school lesson publishers have such materials available for teachers who wish to use them. Many teachers compile a file of their own to have material available for lesson illustration and development.

PROJECTED STILL PICTURES

There are a great many filmstrips in use today. A church can profitably begin its instructional aids library with a collection of some of the best of these. Filmstrips are available for teacher training, for Old Testament and New Testament studies, and for almost every major aspect of Christian teaching. Other forms of projected still pictures include slides, opaque projection, and overhead transparencies. Use of the overhead projector is becoming increasingly popular in Christian education.

MOTION PICTURES

In this category there are considerable resources for communicating the gospel and other aspects of Christian living. Normally more expense is involved than in the use of still projection. The use of films must, therefore, be weighed in terms of objectives expected to be achieved as compared with cost. However, the newer film loops and cartridged film are providing materials at lower cost, as well as greatly simplifying film use.

VISUAL BOARDS

Probably the most common type of instructional aid in use in the average church today is the visual board. Under this heading are included such familiar items as the chalkboard, flannelboard, bulletin board, and the newer but extremely versatile "hook 'n loop" board. No classroom should be without a chalkboard, and no teacher should fail to be alert to its great potential. The simple listing of ideas, drawing of stick figures and diagrams, and writing of Scripture references on a chalkboard can enhance practically any teaching situation. Other visual boards represent similar opportunities for improved teaching.

GRAPHICS

Graphics is a descriptive word for charts, diagrams, graphs, cartoons, and map studies. Certainly every teacher teaching a unit on the travels of the Apostle Paul, the life of Christ, or the wanderings of the children of Israel should take advantage of geographical visuals. Less common, but as significantly effective, are charts and diagrams. These can be either purchased or developed personally.

THREE-DIMENSIONAL MATERIALS

Here the focus is on models, exhibits, specimens, and dioramas. Missionaries often use this kind of presentation to give people at home a visual idea of life on the foreign field. Many vacation Bible school courses include three-dimensional materials.

TELEVISION

Video-taping and the use of closed circuit television are becoming increasingly popular in Christian colleges and seminaries, and the development of more economical units has brought it into more regular church use.

GUIDELINES FOR USING INSTRUCTIONAL AIDS

Most teaching aids have wide adaptability, but there are general principles of usage that apply in almost every situation.

The selection of an instructional aid must take into consideration the *age group* with which it is used. For example, it is generally considered that a flannelboard for story telling is most effective for use with children, in that the nature of the figures and the perspectives of scenery relate more to the thought patterns of the childhood years. There is a great deal of flexibility here, however, because some teaching aids can be adapted to almost any age group.

Variety is important in the selection of adequate instructional aids. Occasionally a teacher will have a special interest in a certain tool and overuse it until its effectiveness is greatly dulled. Flannel-graph stories in the children's classes are often subject to this problem.

An understanding of the lesson *objectives* is essential before the proper instructional aids can be selected. Those chosen should provide a definite impetus toward the fulfillment of some part of the lesson goal, rather than merely add interest to the lesson.

Teachers should always *preview* films, slides, and filmstrips before their use. The preview is not merely to determine the material's fitness for the teaching situation. It also facilitates lesson planning as the teacher prepares his class for what they will view, and then structures the follow-up to develop and apply its meaning.

Every church should develop an instructional aids *library* as a central location for the storing of all teaching aids. This may be part of the regular church library, or it may be set up separately. Proper maintenance and cataloging of all materials are essential.

In a properly functioning instructional aids library, each teacher is given information as to what is available and told how to reserve materials for the time needed. A further service may be instruction in the mechanical use of equipment or the provision of operators.

SUGGESTIONS FOR USE OF SOME INSTRUCTIONAL AIDS

TAPE RECORDINGS

Tape recordings have many varied uses in teaching. Here are some specific ways to use them in your class.

1. By means of recordings bring missionaries, evangelists, and Christian personalities to your class for special occasions or lesson emphasis.

2. Record Christian radio programs and use them as features at group gatherings.

3. Record piano or organ accompaniment for group singing if a piano or organ is not available in your classroom.

4. Make tapes to send to missionaries or class members who have moved away.

5. Record class sessions and take the tapes to shut-ins so that they may benefit by the class as it actually took place.

MURALS

A mural is a series of drawings relating to a common theme. To make a mural, clear off one section of a classroom wall and cover it with white paper. The paper usually used on the tables at church suppers is ideal. Over a period of time, such as a teaching quarter, the students can draw pictures or paste objects to the paper which relate to the lesson series. Pictures for a lesson series on the life of Joseph, for example, could include the coat of many colors, the captivity scene, the various dreams in his life, and other experiences which would be representative of his life story.

OVERHEAD PROJECTION

The overhead projector has become one of the most widely used classroom teaching aids. It is operated from the front of the room and allows the teacher to face the class at all times. It does not require a dark room.

The teacher can use prepared transparencies or write-on sheets or a roll of clear acetate. Transparency pens (available in most office or school supply stores) are used to mark on the transparency material. These pens are available in a wide variety of colors and the non-permanent type may be wiped clean with a damp cloth.

Anything that can be drawn on a chalkboard can also be drawn on an overhead projector. Preparation of transparencies also can be done prior to the class.

CHALKBOARD

Green chalkboards are generally preferred over black, and yellow chalk over white. Various drawing instruments can be employed in chalkboard technique, such as a circle maker or music staff marker. The teacher should not be overly concerned about making professional drawings when using the chalkboard. Freehand maps, stick figures, and simple charts can be drawn reasonably well without art experience. Where there is sufficient chalkboard space in the classroom, it is often helpful to allow students to work at the board in drawing maps, writing Scripture verses or using the board for other learning experience.

MAPS

Good Bible maps are available through publishers and bookstores. The creative teacher will also want to make his own maps to emphasize areas of study in which he is directing his class. Map building can also become a class project with class members making a large relief map out of plaster of Paris or papier-maché.

CHARTS

Charts are concerned primarily with the arrangement of words and figures in such an order that the relationship between them can be readily seen. Charts can be made out of cardboard or chart paper. Flip charts are a series of sheets held together by clips, rings, or spiral binding that permit the sheets to be flipped as the lesson progresses.

MODELS

Probably one of the most common models used in Bible teaching is the Old Testament tabernacle. It is not necessary that a model be prepared to absolute scale, although the more accurate it can be made, the more valuable it is for teaching. As with other visuals, models can be either purchased or made by the teacher and class.

DIORAMAS

A diorama is actually another form of a model, with the effect of a three-dimensional picture. A diorama may be as small as a shoebox into which a small "peephole" is cut, allowing the student to look down the box into a three-dimensional display at the other end. Or it may be as large as the entire crucifixion scene covering the whole front of the church.

STUDY PROJECTS

1. Begin a file of pictures which relates to the age group you are teaching or plan to teach. Mount the pictures on colored construction paper and file them topically under such headings as "family," "gifts," "play," "seasons."
2. Make a bulletin board for your classroom or a room in your house. Use inexpensive celotex and cover it with attractive colored burlap. Make a list of the ways which it can be used as a teaching device for the next month.

3. Learn how to operate at least three mechanical teaching devices such as tape recorder, filmstrip projector, slide projector, movie projector, or overhead projector.
4. Suggest at least ten or fifteen different ways that a chalkboard can be used to help visualize the concepts of the lessons you or a friend will be teaching next quarter.
5. Practice making a simple Holy Land map, including the major Bible cities. In the beginning stages you will need to study the maps in your Bible, or a Bible atlas, but practice until you are able to sketch a map without referring to these.

BIBLIOGRAPHY

Edge, Findley B. **Helping the Teacher.** Nashville: Broadman Press, 1959. Chapters 12, 13.

Getz, Gene A. **Audio-Visual Media in Christian Education.** Chicago: Moody Press, 1972.

Jensen, Mary and Andre W. **Audiovisual Idea Book for Churches.** Minneapolis: Augsburg Pub. House, 1974.

Wilson, Ron. **Multimedia Handbook for the Church.** Elgin, IL: D.C. Cook Pub. Co., 1975.

Gathering Teaching Materials

8

What types of teaching materials are there?
Where may the teacher gather teaching materials?
How does the teacher file teaching materials?
What kind of study books does a teacher need?

The dedicated teacher builds an ever-growing collection of materials to enhance his teaching. He knows that a student's learning is not automatic and that it relates largely to the factor of motivation in his mind and life. He attempts, therefore, to secure such motivation through the use of interest-building and idea-conveying materials which both enhance and supplement the actual lesson.

Teaching materials relate to both lesson content and method. Some materials which are gathered by the teacher will find their way right into the lesson. An example of this might be a magazine article on Bible archaeology which bears directly on a Bible passage being studied. On the other hand, an example of materials relating to method would be a picture secured from a current magazine and used to stimulate questions in the classroom. The picture itself may teach no Christian truth, but it is used by the teacher as a contact point to begin a learning experience.

Materials may be viewed in two general categories: verbal and visual. Verbal teaching materials are presented to the class by way of speaking. This would include anecdotes, quotations, supplementary Scripture passages, outlines, and relevant statistics. Visual materials, on the other hand, include pictures, objects, charts, sketches or cartoons, and those things which will be shown to the students as a part of the teaching process.

Among the most important questions regarding teaching materials will be, "Where does the teacher get them?" and, "How does he use them?"

SOURCES OF TEACHING MATERIALS

PERSONAL EXPERIENCES

People who are successful in writing books are usually people who are extremely sensitive to the things around them. They are able to translate ordinary experience into something interesting and meaningful. Lessons and stories appear in the little things that happen to them day by day.

A good teacher develops this kind of sensitivity, too. In a way, all of life may be considered general preparation for teaching. God allows us to have many kinds of experiences—some pleasant, some unpleasant. For the alert teacher, each is a potential teaching point.

BOOKS

The great preacher, W. B. Riley, often said to his students that it was better to go without butter on the table than without books on the shelf. A wealth of helpful literature is available to the teacher of any subject on any level, and there is limitless opportunity for personal growth through reading.

OBSERVING PEOPLE

Observation has long been considered one of the keys to understanding children. There is much to be learned from noting the activities and behavior patterns of almost any age. The alert Christian teacher will constantly see relevant things in the behavior of people that will help him in understanding and illustrating his lesson.

MAGAZINES AND NEWSPAPERS

We are being told that the recent knowledge explosion has produced more information than we have known in all previous history. This has important implications for the Christian teacher who needs to keep aware of what is happening in the world around him. The challenge is not only in gathering illustrations and helps for teaching, but also the strategic importance of relating Christian truth to everyday life in the changing environment in which the student is living right now.

Two important notes should be made about sources. First of all, the average person must *take written notes* on ideas and illustrations in order to retain them for future use. Many teachers find that a notebook just for this is an invaluable aid. Material recorded in this way can later be studied and transferred to a formal file of teaching materials.

A second important note is that material may be gathered without an immediate application in mind. While in many cases the teacher will be looking for specific materials, after teaching a certain lesson he may see a number of places where illustrations or other helps would have greatly improved the lesson. So he begins to look for such material to be used at some future time when he again presents that lesson or a similar one. The teacher should always be alert for general material that is potentially usable. A practical help in this is a basic subject file that provides general categories for which materials should be continually gathered.

SELECTION OF TEACHING MATERIALS

GUIDED BY THE AGE GROUP OF THE STUDENTS

Just as a teacher's methodology and content are related to the age level of the students which he is teaching, so his use of supplementary materials must also be related to age level. A teacher of preschool children is more concerned with gathering teaching pictures and visual materials, whereas a teacher of adults seeks verbal materials to be used in lecture or discussion.

GUIDED BY THE OBJECTIVES OF THE LESSON

To be fully effective, lesson materials must relate to the purposes of a lesson. If the lesson for a given Sunday centers on Christian growth, there is no point in using an object lesson on salvation simply because one is in the file of teaching materials.

TYPES OF TEACHING MATERIAL FILES

As has been suggested, effective use of materials requires some type of filing system. To illustrate filing possibilities, we will list four systems, using specific age group examples as illustration. We will name the teachers of our four sample classes John, Joe, Jill, and Jim.

THE ILLUSTRATION FILE

John teaches a class of junior boys. Since he is concerned in communicating bibical doctrine to them as well as acquainting them with the historical or "story" aspects of the Scriptures, he recognizes the necessity of using verbal illustrations. Sometimes he uses biographical incidents picked up in his reading; sometimes personal experiences; sometimes simple anecdotes. In gathering illustration material, he finds it helpful to use these questions as guidelines:

Is is clear?
Is it interesting?
Is is appropriate?
Is is simple?

In filing his illustrations, this teacher began with a notebook and a simple topical listing, using such common categories as grace, heaven, service, and sin. Later he changed to the folder system in which he has a folder for each topic. The folders are arranged alphabetically in a regular file cabinet drawer. Now, as he finds an effective illustration he transfers it to the proper folder for use when needed.

Illustrations should always have an indication of source so that proper credit can be given where necessary.

THE "IDEA GARDEN"

Joe teaches a senior high class. He has discovered that an effective way of making his teaching relevant to the lives of his teenagers is the use of discussion. So he keeps a file for discussion ideas.

His method of filing is to have an idea page for each lesson. These pages are kept in a notebook for each quarter. As he thinks of discussion questions, he writes them down on the appropriate page and does some preparation in the direction in which he believes the discussion might go. Sometimes he files questions many weeks in advance of the lesson in which he will use them.

This process of study provides a file of ideas that is literally an "idea garden." Ideas are continually being planted for further development and use.

THE PICTURE FILE

Jill has been teaching a kindergarten class for about six months, and she has learned that few things grasp the attention of her four-and five-year olds quicker than an attractive picture. To supplement the Bible pictures in the kindergarten curriculum her church uses, she has become an ardent magazine clipper, cutting out pictures of seasonal landscapes, children in varied activities, family scenes, and practically anything that might have use with her class. After the picture is carefully cut and trimmed, she mounts it on colored construction paper which blends with the color tones of the picture and then puts it in the proper subject file folder. Whenever a picture has been used in her class, she marks the date on the back of the picture to keep a record of its use.

THE OUTLINE AND STUDY NOTES FILE

Jim teaches an elective class in the Gospel of John for young adults. He hasn't had formal classroom instruction in New Testament studies, but he has become a dedicated student of all the available literature on his subject. He borrowed books from his pastor, and made extensive notes. A series of articles on the Gospel of John in an evangelical periodical was carefully clipped and filed.

For his purpose this teacher uses a textual file. It is based on twenty-one file folders—one for each chapter in the Gosepl of John. Into it go outlines, illustrations, notes, and any material that bears on the content of a particular chapter.

THE TEACHER'S LIBRARY

A teacher's personal library may be his most valuable possession. Careful selection of books and good reading habits will prove a rewarding experience for the conscientious teacher.

THE VALUES OF A PERSONAL LIBRARY

There is now a wealth of written material available for helping the Christian teacher in his task. Consider the following values of a good basic library.

Good books are essential for an enriched teaching ministry, and help keep the teacher from staleness by providing fresh ideas and insights.

Good books open to the teacher the heritage of history and the experience of others. Careful reading can often keep him from repeating errors in living and teaching.

Good books give the teacher access to information he may not have had time or opportunity to study in formal education. Few lay teachers in Sunday school, for example, have had formal instruction in archaeology. Yet, careful reading can provide understanding and material in this field that will open up meaning for many passages in both the Old and New Testaments.

THE SELECTION OF BOOKS

A teacher's shelves should be stocked with good source books. Purchase reference works such as Bible dictionaries, concordances, and introductions. These are books that will be used again and again, rather than just read once and forgotten.

Special bibliography listings often provide publication and cost information, as well as recommendations. Helpful book reviews appear in most evangelical periodicals. Denominational headquarters or Christian bookstores can often provide suggestions.

STUDY PROJECTS

1. Begin to build a picture file, starting with ten basic subject categories that relate to the age level in which you are interested.
2. Make a lesson notebook for the next quarter for a class you are attending or teaching. Have a section for each lesson and begin now to record material that will be helpful in teaching.
3. Develop a list of ten books relating to your teaching interest that you might add to your personal library within the next year.
4. Clip at least one article that might have use in your teaching from each day's edition of your newspaper for one week.
5. Begin next Sunday to take notes on your pastor's sermons and file them in some kind of textual or topical file.

BIBLIOGRAPHY

Benson, Clarence H. **Teaching Techniques.** Rev. ed. Wheaton, IL: Evangelical Teaching Training Assn., 1974. Chapter 6.

Ryan, Roy H. **Planning and Leading Bible Study.** Nashville: Local Church Education Board of Discipleship of the United Methodist Church, 1973.

Preparing

To

Teach

9

What are basic steps in lesson preparation?
Why is prayer important for the teacher?
What is involved in practical Bible study?
How should the teacher's lesson quarterly be used in preparation?
What is a lesson plan and how is it used?

All of life can be considered general preparation for teaching. However, there are also specific preparation steps involved in effective teaching.

PRAYER FOUNDATION

There is no substitute for prayer as preparation for Christian teaching. Recognition of God and dependence on his guidance are essential in any teaching that has spiritual goals.

WE ARE URGED TO PRAY

In I Thessalonians 5:17, the Apostle Paul commands believers to "pray without ceasing." Jesus told his disciples: "Verily, verily,

I say unto you, whatsoever ye shall ask the Father in my name, he will give it you. Hitherto have ye asked nothing in my name: ask, and ye shall receive, that your joy may be full" (John 16:23, 24).

WE NEED TO PRAY

Few teachers have not come to the place where they felt a need for wisdom beyond their own in their work with students. The encouragement of James 1:5 NIV is: "If any of you lacks wisdom, he should ask God, who gives generously to all without finding fault, and it will be given to him."

Concerned for the ministry of teaching, and burdened with the needs of our students, we need to come often to our God for his wisdom and strength. The teacher would do well to read carefully John 17 for Christ's example of prayer intercession.

BIBLE STUDY

Bible study to prepare for teaching involves understanding as fully as possible the portion to be taught. Here is a simple six-step plan for inductive-type study.

READ WITH OPEN MIND

Come to the unit with a mind open to the Holy Spirit's leading. (The "unit" may be an entire book, a chapter, or a smaller portion of a chapter.) Read slowly and carefully, trying to picture yourself in the writer's position. Some teachers find it helpful to augment their reading by using various translations or paraphrases. The passage being studied should be read many times so that the full meaning of what is in the text finds its way into the heart and mind of the teacher.

LIST SIGNIFICANT DETAILS

Almost all effective study is done with pen and paper ready to record information acquired through the study. *Proper names* should be listed and followed by the identity of the people who come into the passage. Furthermore, identify all *places* by using up-to-date Bible maps to locate the geographical references. *Events* represent a third category of facts. What happened in the passage and in what sequence did the happenings take place? Finally, try to determine when each event took place. A *time* reference might represent anything from the century in which a certain Old Testament event occurred, to the time of day at which our Lord died.

STUDY BY PARAGRAPHS

Not every Bible divides chapters by paragraphs. The New International Version is a translation that does use paragaraphs and there are other paragraph editions, such as a King James edition by the American Bible Society.

For each paragraph in your study unit, write the key thought or theme of the paragraph. Give the paragraph a title. The title may be similar to the theme but will usually be briefer. This study exercise will emphasize the basic thought within each paragraph, as well as indicate the continuity of thought between paragraphs. Watch for repetition of words, phrases, and ideas.

SEEK MEANING

It is the *meaning* of facts which, when believed, can produce supernatural life in the individual. For example, the fact that a person called Christ died in Palestine is not the major issue. The meaning of the crucifixion lies in why he died and for whom he died.

STUDY THE CONTEXTUAL RELATIONSHIP

The principle of context is important in the interpretation of Scripture. Here you attempt to ascertain the relationship of a particular unit to other units in the chapter, other chapters in the book, and other books in the Bible. Whole units are studied rather than small unrelated facts, and one part is allowed to help explain the other parts.

DETERMINE THE CENTRAL MESSAGE

In determining the message of a given passage, the teacher considers the progress of thought, as well as the unit itself.

When the teacher has inductively studied the Bible, he is ready to gather additional information from other resources.

STUDY HELPS

THE TEACHER'S QUARTERLY

The teacher's quarterly (or teacher's helps), normally included with published Sunday school literature, can be very helpful in preparing to teach. When it becomes a substitute for adequate preparation, however, it is a hindrance. Remember that the lesson quarterly is just like a Bible commentary. It belongs in the preparation section of your teaching and not in the presentation.

Normally, teachers' quarterlies include the following preparation helps:

Introduction to the lesson
Outline of the passage under consideration
Commentary on verses of difficult interpretation
Illustrations
Cross references which lead to related Bible passages
Ideas on application and expanded development

REFERENCE BOOKS

A Bible dictionary is particularly helpful in determining meanings of terms, location of places, usage of names, and other factual information. Some helpful Bible dictionaries are the *New Bible Dictionary, Unger's Bible Dictionary,* and the *Zondervan Pictorial Bible Encyclopedia.*

COMMENTARIES

Commentaries might be categorized in two general areas: *devotional* and *exegetical* (interpretive). In the first category would be works by Adam Clarke, Matthew Henry, and Bishop Ellicott. Devotional commentaries of this type are generally easier to handle than the exegetical in that they place less emphasis on the interpretation of the original languages and concentrate more on materials related to Christian living.

Exegetical commentaries will be helpful for the trained teacher seeking clarity of Bible passages for his own enrichment and the teaching of adults.

RELATED SOURCES

The effective teacher always will be looking for information and materials which will enhance his teaching ministry. Resources relating to Bible history, geography, and archaeology, for example, can add greatly to effective teaching. The teacher's own files are also potential treasuries of teaching helps, if he faithfully collects resource materials.

LESSON OUTLINE

Learning takes place more readily when the presentation of the teacher is organized and well-structured. For this purpose, a lesson outline is a vital aid.

USE PROPER OUTLINE FORM

This means making points grammatically parallel and developing progression from the beginning of the outline to the end.

Standard outline symbols follow a I, A, l, b pattern. However, whether one outlines using Roman numerals, capital letters, or a combination of numbers and letters such as l a, the important factor is consistency. Follow the same pattern throughout the outline, keeping in mind that an A requires at least a B, and a l requires a 2.

BE CONCISE AND SIMPLE

It is not necessary when outlining a lesson to use full sentences. Sometimes a single word will suffice. The important matter is that the outline have meaning for the user and fulfill its purpose as a teaching aid.

USE CONVENIENT SIZE PAPER

The size of your Bible is the guideline. The outline sheet should fit into the Bible without extending on any side. For this purpose it might be trimmed to about ¼" smaller than the Bible page to provide for both neat appearance and easy handling. Outline cards, if used, should be able to be conveniently held and turned.

LESSON PLAN

A final step in preparing to teach is to put into written form all of the procedures and information which you are going to use in a given class period. This is called a *lesson plan,* and it includes the lesson outline. A lesson plan may take different forms, but there are items that are basic to almost every plan. The example below is a lesson plan which appears in the E.T.T.A. book, *Teaching Techniques.* While you may not include all of the items listed each time you teach, the outline indicates the major points to be considered.

Lesson title
Scripture
Memory verse
Central truth
Lesson aim
Lesson outline
Approach (create a readiness for learning)

Body (include a selection of teaching methods, audiovisuals, questions and illustrations)
Conclusion (apply the lesson to life)
Possible assignments for the following lesson
Evaluation of the class session (to be filled in after the lesson has been taught)[1]

Remember that the effective teacher plans for almost all the learning experiences that will take place during the class period. He plans, for example, to include participation in the form of questions or discussions. He tries to think ahead and consider what questions the students might ask him about difficult or controversial passages in the lesson. He also previews the entire class period as much as possible in his own mind. He visualizes himself beginning the lesson, and carrying it on through. He may even practice stating certain questions which will be keys to discussion. In short, he uses every means for adequate preparation, rather than leaving learning to chance.

It is said that one enjoys doing whatever one does well and that one learns to do well whatever one enjoys. This certainly can and should be applied to teaching.

NOTES

1. Clarence H. Benson, *Teaching Techniques* (Wheaton, IL: Evangelical Teacher Training Association, rev. ed. 1974), p.55.

STUDY PROJECTS

1. Do an inductive analysis of John 15, using the steps suggested in the BIBLE STUDY section.
2. Outline the 15th chapter of the Gospel of John, utilizing the information which you have gathered in STUDY PROJECT #1 above.
3. Write a lesson plan for a Sunday school lesson on John 15; again utilize the information in STUDY PROJECT #1 and STUDY PROJECT #2.
4. Use a Bible dictionary to do a thorough study of Acts 1.

BIBLIOGRAPHY

Benson, Clarence H. **Teaching Techniques.** Rev. ed. Wheaton, IL: Evangelical Teacher Training Association, 1974. Chapter 7.

Edge, Findley B. **Helping the Teacher.** Nashville: Broadman Press, 1959. Chapters 2-4.

_____.**Teaching for Results.** Nashville: Broadman Press, 1956. Chapters 5-11.

Richards, Lawrence O. **Creative Bible Teaching.** Chicago: Moody Press, 1970. Chapters 21-24.

Creative Teaching

How does creativity relate to teaching?
What are the qualities of a creative teacher?
How may a teacher develop creativity in himself?
How may a teacher develop creativity in his students?

While creativity is a currently popular term among educators, the concept of newness and freshness which it conveys has always been basic to good teaching. Creativity should be the living experience of the teacher whose life has been touched by the Savior and is directed by the Spirit of God. The effects of creativity should be seen in lesson preparation and presentation if the life throb of today is to permeate our thinking.

DEFINING CREATIVE TEACHING
RESPONSE TO CHALLENGE
There are few challenges in any realm of life which are as great

as that of classroom teaching. This challenge is further magnified in the context of Christian teaching. The goals of evangelism, Christian growth, service training, and Christlike behavior constantly demand fresh approches and response. A creative response to the challenge may include new planning procedures, fresh ways to elicit the interest of every student, better organization of the subject matter, or greater variety in teaching methods.

CONSTANT DEVELOPMENT OF IDEAS

Creativity might be defined as a quality which causes the teacher to develop original and imaginative ideas in teaching. Actually, ideas verbalized or visualized in classroom work can be just as dynamic and significant as ideas which find form in the work of artists and musicians. The teacher who brings fresh insight and approach to the teaching situation is truly a creative artist.

THE USE OF IMAGINATION

Imagination is usually associated with storytelling in Christian education. However, dedicated imagination has a place in all areas of teaching. The teacher, for example, who is able to visualize the classroom as Daniel's lions' den for juniors or a Roman forum for high school discussions adds a creative dimension to his teaching. Picturing the Apostle Paul writing the book of Philippians in a Roman jail brings new prospective to a study of that book. Based on biblical facts, imagination brings interest and life to the biblical lesson.

There may be some who feel that the use of imagination is beyond their ability. However, there is considerable encouragement on the possibility of developing creative imagination. Dr. Ralph J. Hallman states:

> . . . creativity can be taught. It can be taught because the process of being creative is the process of developing one's self as a personality. It is the process of unfettering the chains of habit, routine, and repression. It is the process of shaping one's surroundings, or relating one's self productively to others; it is the process of identifying one's self and defining one's own existence. This is the central problem of creativity; it is also the central problem of education.[1]

THE APPLICATION OF CREATIVITY

Creativity remains an abstract concept until it is applied to classroom procedure. These are suggestions on principles of application.

CREATIVITY IN METHOD

Creativity in method has many applications but most of all it means variety. The creative teacher will not allow himself to become stereotyped in his teaching methodology. His methods will vary. He will combine methods. He will introduce ways of communicating which have never been demonstrated to his class before, and he will seek by reading, conference, and experiment to keep his class presentation fresh and invigorating.

CREATIVITY IN ROOM FACILITIES

The physical features of the classroom offer definite opportunity for creativity. For example, the use of circles, semi-circles, small groups, or perhaps the getting rid of desk and chairs entirely in some children's departments, may bring a fresh sense of creativity to the whole classroom setting. It could conceivably revolutionize the attitude of students in that room toward the teaching hour. Similarly, the use of pictures, bulletin boards, and fresh paint offers potential creative opportunity.

CREATIVITY IN ASSIGNMENTS

Few would argue against the benefit of having the student prepare for a class through some type of outside study. There is considerable problem, however, on how such outside study can be motivated in church study. Here is a challenge for the creative teacher. He is not satisfied with a casual "read the chapter," but will attempt to establish inner motivation and desire.

QUALITIES OF A CREATIVE TEACHER

Creativity is not present to the same degree in every individual, although nearly everyone has capacity for it. While there may be a close correlation between high creativity and above average intelligence, intelligence is not necessarily the primary ingredient of creativity. Creativity has several common qualities:

ENTHUSIASM

Enthusiasm is not to be equated with noise or mere physical activity. Creativity in the Christian teacher means first of all dynamic relationship to God and to His Word. Out of this comes enthusiasm for his teaching and a contagious interest in the things of God.

OPEN-MINDEDNESS

The highly creative person has an open-mindedness to experience. He does not interpret each statement and act of his students by preconceived conclusions. He is willing to allow temporary failure on the part of others in their search for proper application of the truths of God. He seeks new solutions to old problems. He relates old principles to new problems in new ways and with new emphasis. He applies the wisdom of the past to the challenge of the future by a willingness to listen to others and help them find for themselves the answers they seek.

SENSITIVITY

The creative person, whether artist, musician, or teacher, is sensitive to his surroundings. He is observant of sounds, colors, people, and the daily events of life that surround us. Again, this is an ability that can be cultivated by the teacher who desires to improve his creative powers.

PERSONAL GROWTH

The growth process for the Christian is continuous, and so is the learning process for a teacher. There is never a time when the Christian teacher knows all that he needs to know about the Word of God or about the teaching process. There is never a time when he knows all there is to know about his students. The dedicated teacher is constantly growing in his abilities, and his creative potential grows with him.

DEVELOPING CREATIVITY

Practices which encourage creativity ought to engage the mind of the teacher regularly. Let us consider some of these exercises:

DEVELOP A GOOD READING PROGRAM

One can increase creativity through vocabulary and thought patterns developed by effective reading. Good reading involves both methods and content. Underlining, taking notes, and other methods of conserving reading results multiply the effectiveness of the reading. For reading content, choose stimulating books on teaching, as well as keeping up with helpful material in Christian periodicals.

APPLY PROBLEM-SOLVING TECHNIQUES

The creative person seeks to develop ways to approach and handle problems. A good problem-solving approach usually involves isolating the problem, suggesting solutions, evaluating solutions, selecting the best solution, and putting it into practice on an experimental basis.

USE "BRAINSTORMING"APPROACH

Quantity often provides a base for quality. As a teacher by himself or with others lists all the ideas that come spontaneously and immediately on a particular subject, he exercises his mental abilities. Then, as he is able to dip into a resource of numerous ideas on a given question, he has a wider field to work with than just casual study might produce.

PRACTICE DEFERRED JUDGMENT

Waiting to judge an idea until it has been given a hearing creates a healthy climate for idea production. The teacher who would be creative is one who listens to ideas regardless of his own bias or initial reaction. He never shuts off his own thinking on the basis that his ideas aren't worthwhile or won't work. Ultimately, of course, the value of ideas must be determined, but they must first be permitted expression.

ENCOURAGING CREATIVITY IN STUDENTS

The teacher who is aware of creative possibilities usually seeks to develop creativity on the part of his students. He wants to encourage imaginative and original ideas, and have his students ultimately be able to solve their own problems through the proper application of the principles of the Word of God. Several qualities should characterize the teaching situation if such creativity is going to be developed in students.

EMPATHY ON THE PART OF THE TEACHER

Attempt to see things from a student's viewpoint. An old Indian proverb suggests that no Indian brave should comment on his brother's behavior until he has lived in his moccasins for at least a week. The teacher who would help the students grow must know some of the home problems and difficulties of his student, as well as having some understanding of the characteristics of the age group with which he is working.

VARIETY IN THE TEACHING SITUATION

As already indicated, variety is one of the observable characteristics of creative teaching. The teacher who would stir his students cannot just transmit the same notes or use the same approach week after week. There must be change, there must be freshness in the classroom situation.

TOLERANCE IN CLASSROOM WORK

Growth in student creativity is encouraged by a classroom atmosphere that allows for mistakes. The wise teacher seeks to guide the student toward corrected thinking rather than abruptly cutting off any discussion that is not fully correct. Such a cooperative learning process, where the teacher neither dominates nor discourages classroom activity, develops student interest and initiative.

EVALUATION BY THE STUDENT

Students must be taught how to test ideas and establish true values. This involves such areas as correct perspective on peer group pressures and understanding the application of Scriptures to life situations. Eventually, the student must establish his own pattern of living and make independent decisions. The teacher points toward this by creative teaching that introduces real life situations and guides the student toward his own biblically sound solutions. In this process the teacher by availability and conference serves as a resource person. He also encourages the use of all pertinent materials.

CREATIVITY AND THE ETERNAL WORD

There is great difference between the educational ideology of evangelical Christianity and that of secularism. It is a crucial matter, for example, whether truth is absolute or largely relative. Has God spoken authoritatively on some issues, or does each generation determine truth for itself?

For the Christian teacher, creativity can never exceed the bounds of God's revealed truth, for the most significant event of history is that God has spoken and revealed himself to man. Unguided creativity may replace divine values with human values. Thus, while the Christian teacher wants to be creative, he keeps his creativity within the bounds of the Word of God and the Holy Spirit's direction of his intellect and imaginative capacities.

NOTES
1. *Educational Theory,* Vol. XVI, January, 1964.

STUDY PROJECTS
1. Select a problem or question which you are facing in your teaching. Then endeavor to list every conceivable way that the problem could be solved. Remember not to criticize or discuss any possible solution until you complete the list. Now evaluate the suggestions to determine the ones that are most practical.
2. Review the qualities of a creative teacher as given in this chapter and evaluate your own status.
3. Taking a specific teaching situation (your own or one you observe), write at least one suggestion for creative improvement on method, room arrangement, assignments, student involvement.
4. Carry a notebook and pen with you for one week wherever you go. Consciously keep alert to, and record, ideas that could encourage and aid your imaginative powers for teaching. At the end of the week, evaluate the ideas recorded in terms of their value for teaching.
5. Study John 4 and record whatever you feel represents a creative approach. Do the same for other teaching examples in the New Testament.

BIBLIOGRAPHY
Bingham, Robert E. **New Ways of Teaching the Old Story.** Nashville: Broadman Press, 1970.

Edge, Findley B. **Teaching for Results.** Nashville: Broadman Press, 1956, Chapter 4.

LeBar, Lois. **Education That is Christian.** Old Tappan, NJ: Fleming H. Revell Co. 1958.

Richards, Lawrence O. **Creative Bible Teaching.** Chicago: Moody Press, 1970.

Zuck, Roy B. **Spiritual Power in Your Teaching.** Rev. ed. Chicago: Moody Press, 1972.

Relating Truth
To
Life

What kind of teaching hinders the translation of truth to life?
How can the truth of a lesson be extended beyond the classroom?
What kind of assignments can be made to relate truth to life?
How can the classroom be related to the home?

Christ said to his disciples, "If ye know these things, happy are ye if ye do them" (John 13:17). Effective Christian teaching can usually be evaluated by the growth it produces in the lives of students.

In his *Taxonomy of Educational Objectives,* Benjamin Bloom indicates that there are six levels in learning: knowledge, comprehension, application, analysis, synthesis, and evaluation. [1] Each of these increases in value and each succeeding one incorporates the levels that precede it. One of the familiar problems in teaching is that we are content to stop at knowledge level when we should press on to comprehension, application, and the higher levels of learning.

TEACHING IS MORE THAN TELLING

Someone once cynically defined a lecture as the process by which information is transferred from the notes of the teacher to the notes of the student without having passed through the heads of either. One of the major emphases of this book has been that good communication is not only in one direction, nor is it merely transmission of facts.

THE NEED FOR INTERACTION

Interaction, as opposed to one-way teaching, not only enables the student to better comprehend during the actual teaching-learning process, but also provides opportunities for him to relate this truth to given situations. The questions he asks in class may be motivated by actual life situations. The biblical answers, therefore, find immediate application to life.

THE NEED FOR RELEVANCE

The Bible itself is not irrelevant. However, there is a need for bridge-building between the truth of the Word of God and the student's experiences. The fact that the Bible is relevant to the student's life is not sufficient. He must recognize the relevance and understand how biblical principles can be applied to life. This application to life is a process and not a single event.

THE NEED FOR MOTIVATION

For teaching to become more than mere telling, the student must be motivated to do something with the lesson. Recognition of some kind is basic in almost all motivation, and the effective teacher encourages his students in every way possible.

OBSTACLES TO RELATING TRUTH

A realistic appraisal of teaching recognizes that not every student wants to relate truth to his life. Further, some who might want to apply the truth, have difficulty because of problems involved in the process. It is the teacher's responsibility to recognize such problems and alleviate them as much as possible.

PERSONAL INERTIA

Much of the Bible knowledge which Christians possess is secondhand. It is composed of interpretations and ideas gained through listening to preachers and teachers and reading Christian literature. These are fine sources of information. However, they are not to be substitutes for the personal Bible study that should be a part of the lives of all Christians.

Some do not study the Bible because they do not know how. The teacher should instruct these in techniques of personal Bible study. On the other hand, there may be a neglect which is simply the product of the natural mind. Learning takes work, and some do not choose to work. The need for motivation is obvious here and it is a challenge to the teacher's creativity.

INTELLECTUAL BARRIERS

Every teacher will have in his class at some time students lacking mental capabilities for the task at hand. With these the teacher will have to exercise patience, and work on a very individualized basis. Usually, it will be difficult for these to recognize the application of truth, and, therefore, the reproduction of truth in his life takes more time and effort on the part of the teacher.

LACK OF COMMITMENT

Learning, for the Christian, involves relationship to the will of God. When one seeks to do the will of God, he faces commitment to Christ's claim on his life. Here the problem of sinful nature enters in, and the Christian teacher will need the resources of the Holy Spirit to help his students develop spiritual strength. Indeed, the glory of Christian teaching is that the Spirit of God works in and through the teacher to meet the spiritual needs of students.

LACK OF HOME ENCOURAGEMENT

Parental support is extremely important to the teacher of children and youth. Memorization of verses, preparaton for class discussion, and general orientation toward the importance of the class, all need to be fostered in the home. Further, the teacher must work to avoid conflicting standards between church and home in the mind of the student. Therefore, there must be the constant strengthening of ties between the class and the home.

PROJECTING TRUTH BEYOND THE CLASSROOM

Since the Word of God is the authoritative center of curriculum in Christian education, constant effort must be made to guide men and women, boys and girls to study the Bible for themselves. Such study will go far beyond the classroom if it is to be related to life.

INDIVIDUAL STUDY

The teacher's own enthusiasm is an important factor in how much study the student does outside of class. The goal is to make class material meaningful, and show students the value of further study in their own lives. This involves a clear understanding of the use of assignments for home study and attractive presentation of such assignments. It can also mean personal advice by phone, the lending of books, and other help on the part of the teacher. Finally, he must expect the student to do well and then give recognition and credit for work that is well done.

ASSISTING HOMES

There are specific things which the classroom teacher can encourage in relating the work in his class to the home life of the students.

Family Devotions

The teacher of children, in assigning Scripture verses, might emphasize how the family can and should study the Bible and pray together. This will be communicated even more effectively if the teacher is also able to speak to the parents along these lines. The teacher of adults has the opportunity to emphasize family devotions. Perhaps a format for family devotions can be explained in class.

Parent-Teacher Fellowships

The public school system has long placed high premium on its PTA organizations. Many Christian day schools have organized parent-teacher fellowships. Church educational programs also will find some form of parent-teacher relationship helpful. If scheduled meetings are arranged, opportunity can be provided to explain the objectives and curriculum of the class and the relationships of truths taught to home life. Parents' cooperation should be solicited with the explanation of what they can do to assist classroom teaching efforts. This involvement will benefit both students and the homes from which they come.

PERSONAL CONTACT

There is probably no more effective way of tying the classroom to the home than by the personal visitation of the teacher. The genuinely concerned teacher will seek to visit in the home of each class member to help them relate classroom teaching.

HELPS TO RELATING TRUTHS

Some basic suggestions can be summarized on the matter of life-relatedness and teaching. The teacher who desires to focus teaching on Christian living will find it helpful to consider and use these suggestions:

SPECIFIC APPLICATIONS

Make life-related applications of Bible truth through the use of life-situation illustrations and student involvement. It is necessary that the student see himself in the situation. This can sometimes be done through the telling of a life-situation story. Often it is accomplished by engaging the student in discussion of life problems and then leading him to biblical principles regarding those problems and their solution.

PROJECTS AND REPORTS

Assign projects and reports that will lead the students to put into practice things they have learned. This type of home study has value beyond the project's immediate benefits.

WEEKDAY CONTACTS

Follow up classroom work by observing and helping students in their regular weekday activities. The teacher who desires to fully communicate with his students in the classroom will make a genuine effort to be with those students outside of the classroom. This includes participation in group activities and service projects.

HOME RELATIONSHIPS

Carefully relate the lessons presented to the home. This has special application to the Christian home, for church and home should have common spiritual objectives.

Relating truth to life is a vital part of the Christian teacher's ministry. All teaching should change lives, but Christian teaching has the advantage of the power of the eternal Word and the Holy Spirit to accomplish its task.

NOTES

1. Benjamin S. Bloom (ed), *Taxonomy of Educational Objectives* (New York: David McKay Co., 1956).

STUDY PROJECTS

1. Suggest ways to assist students in overcoming the obstacles to learning mentioned in this chapter.
2. List at least five life-related follow-up activities for one lesson theme.
3. Plan a parent-teacher program for a specific Sunday school class. Include meeting schedule, place, time, programs, and promotion.
4. Plan for a visitation program by a Sunday school class, indicating how it should be organized and how large a part the student could play.
5. Write a one-paragraph analysis of the statement "Teaching is more than telling."

BIBLIOGRAPHY

Benson, Clarence H. **Teaching Techniques.** Rev. ed. Wheaton, IL: Evangelical Teacher Training Association, 1974. Chapter 11.

Edge, Findley B. **Teaching for Results.** Nashville: Broadman Press, 1956. Chapter 9.

Richards, Lawrence O. **Creative Bible Teaching.** Chicago: Moody Press, 1970.

Rood, Wayne R. **The Art of Teaching Christianity.** Nashville: Abingdon Press, 1968.

Evaluating

Our

Teaching

What is meant by educational evaluation?
How can a teacher construct good tests?
What kinds of objective tests can be used?
How does informal evaluation help?
What is the students' part in teacher evaluation?

Evaluation is the process of determining to what extent we have achieved our goals. To evaluate we must first assume that goals have been established. And, secondly, we must recognize there are some goals that cannot be measured objectively. This is largely true of goals of spiritual growth and behavior.

Good suggestions for evaluation of teaching are found in Rozell's *Talks on Sunday School Teaching*. He suggests teachers ask themselves:

Is the class growing in attendance?
Are students growing in participation in the teaching period?
Is the class growing in enthusiasm for Bible study?
Are members growing in the making of right choices and in Christian convictions?
Are students changing others instead of being changed by them? [1]

Note that the general principle involved in these questions is the matter of growth and change.

Three types of evaluation should be considered by the Christian teacher: written tests, observation, and records.

EVALUTION THROUGH WRITTEN TESTS

One means of evaluation is measurement through testing. Tests provide information for the teacher on how well students have gained knowledge through his teaching. They are means of student evaluation that have a number of basic forms.

TYPES OF WRITTEN TESTS

Multiple Choice Tests

A multiple choice test is one in which the student reads the question and then selects his answer from a list of alternatives (usually four) which the teacher provides with the question.

Example: The Holy Spirit descended upon the disciples during the celebration of which Jewish feast?

    a. Passover   c. Tabernacles
    b. Pentecost   d. Dedication

In constructing multiple choice questions it is well to observe these rules:

1. Avoid listing obviously wrong alternatives.
2. Make sure that one of the alternatives is distinctly better than the others.
3. Place all of the essential information in the question.
4. Be sure that each of the alternatives grammatically fits into the sentence.

Since there is a high degree of objectivity in this type of evaluation little subjective judgment is needed on the part of the teacher. Many professional testing centers consider the multiple choice test one of the best kind of objective tests for class use.

Completion Tests

These make a statement, leaving out a crucial part, and substituting for that part a blank space or spaces. The student's task is to fill in the missing word or words.

Here is a sample:

When the Apostle Paul was converted he was on his way to the city of..

In constructing completion tests observe the following guidelines:

1. Be sure there is only one correct answer that can be placed in the blank.

2. Try to place the blank near the end of the statement rather than near the beginning.

3. Provide whatever information the student needs to understand the question clearly. For example, in the sample question, the word "city" is essential lest the student put down the name of a province, or even a country and still be correct.

True-False Tests

The true or false test is one in which a statement is made and the student indicates by marking whether the statement is true or false.

Example: James and John were the sons of Zecharias...................

True and false tests are subject to guessing and do not always provide the best measurement of knowledge. The teacher who uses them should note the following:

1. Make sure the statement is clearly either true or false.

2. Keep the statement simple so that only one basic idea is presented.

3. Recognize the deficiences of this type of test, and avoid using it as the total means of evaluation.

Matching Tests

Like the multiple choice test, the matching test provides complete test material. The student's task is to match words or statements to the correctly related words or statements.

Here is a sample:

1. Paul ....   a - wrote the books of Acts
2. Peter ....   b - was the last disciple to die
3. John ....   c - saw a vision of a sheet descending
                                 from heaven
                 d - escaped from a town by being lowered
                                 over the wall in a basket

In using matching tests the teacher should observe the following rules:

1. Each list should concentrate on only one subject. For example, it could concern names of people or information on dates, but not a combination of dates and names in any one series.

2. Limit the number of matching items in any one series to less than ten.

3. The number of possible answers should exceed the number of base words or statements.

4. Clearly define the basis on which answers will be considered correct.

Essay

In an essay test the student responds to the question by writing the answer in his own words. This permits the student to indicate his personal grasp of the subject. The grading process becomes somewhat subjective and involves more time than the average objective test. Here is a sample essay question:

Write a paragraph describing how a person becomes a Christian. Support your answer with Scripture passages. (You may use your Bible in answering this question.)

In preparing an essay test observe the following guidelines:

1. Make the questions as specific as possible so that the students' answers can be evaluated specifically.

2. Allow the student adequate time for answering the question.

CHARACTERISTICS OF GOOD WRITTEN TESTS

Knowledge is much easier to measure objectively than understanding, and yet understanding is a higher level of learning than knowledge. The effective teacher will be concerned with measuring both of these, and measuring them as objectively as possible. In doing so, he will observe the characteristics of good written tests.

Objectivity

Objectivity in testing knowledge is not difficult to attain because one can ask for specific information, such as the age of Moses when he died, or the name of the man who was swallowed by the great fish. It becomes more difficult, however, to test the student's *understanding* objectively. Such testing involves setting a new situation for the student, something which he did not encounter in class, and getting him to apply principles that were taught.

Clarity
The question should not be ambiguous, or capable of more than one correct interpretation.

Comprehensiveness
A test is comprehensive when it touches on each of the major areas of the unit studied.

Validity
A test is valid if it tests what it is supposed to test. If, for example, we are testing for the student's understanding of salvation, the result of our test should actually indicate this information.

EVALUATION THROUGH OBSERVATION
As already indicated, evaluation is more than measurement by written testing forms. If learning is to result in change, then change observed in the life of the students is one indication of effective communication from teacher to student.

A large part of evaluation through observation relates to the subjective impressions received by the teacher when he is with a student. These impressions concern attitude and behavior, as well as generalized impressions concerning knowledge and comprehension.

There is also a more formal approach to observation. In this approach the teacher establishes the developments or changes he would like to see, and then seeks to observe the students in situations where such changes are most likely to show themselves.

EVALUATION THROUGH RECORDS
The teacher who is concerned about his students' progress will find a good record system valuable. Good records concern more than attendance. They include such matters as the student's class achievements, personal interests, and indications of spiritual growth. Some information can be translated into graph form and the student's development charted over a period of time.

RECORDS SHOULD BE PRACTICAL
Practicality includes establishing a standard record system that will be both understandable and convenient for those who use it.

The forms themselves can be simple, but they must provide the desired information in legible manner. For the teacher's personal records, a notebook or card index is recommended. Many Sunday school publishers offer such materials.

RECORDS SHOULD BE KEPT UP-TO-DATE

Once records fall behind, it is most difficult to catch up on the entries. It is best to have a regular entry time, such as immediately after the class session.

RECORDS SHOULD BE ACCESSIBLE

Records are of little value if merely kept but not used. Having them accessible, therefore, is vital in encouraging use. This refers to general Sunday school records as well as teacher's records.

TEACHER EVALUATION

The conscientious teacher recognizes that evaluation of teaching is incomplete until he has also secured evaluation of himself as a teacher. One approach to this is through the students, either by anonymous questionnaires or by informal conferences. The more mature the student, the more helpful such evaluation usually becomes. The teacher can also judge his teaching by such means as tape recording and the evaluation of a qualified observer.

Here is a list of suggested questions for the teacher to consider or have others apply to his teaching:

1. Did the lesson show organization?
2. Did the teacher produce interest in the subject and create desire for learning?
3. Was the teacher personally interested and enthusiastic?
4. Did the teaching produce helpful class participation?
5. Did the teacher demonstrate working knowledge of the subject?
6. Did the teacher encourage students to express opinions whether or not they differed with his own?
7. Did the teaching point toward practical relationships between biblical truth and life?
8. Was there orderliness without repressiveness in the classroom?
9. Was the relationship between teacher and students one of friendliness and respect?
10. Were assignments clearly given so that students understood what was expected?

NOTES

1. Ray Rozell, *Talks On Sunday School Teaching* (Grand Rapids: Zondervan Pub. House, 1956), Chapter 10.

STUDY PROJECTS

1. Using an actual lesson, develop five multiple choice, five completion, and five matching questions, following the suggestions noted in this chapter for test construction.
2. Using the same lesson as in the previous project, write five related essay questions.
3. If you are a teacher or a parent, list all the ways in which you carried on informal observation of children or young people during the past week. Think about how this observation can be related to educational objectives.
4. Obtain a copy of a test which has been used in church work within the past year and evaluate it on the basis of the characteristics of good written tests described in this chapter.
5. Using only available records, seek to build a meaningful picture of a student who has been active in your Sunday school for several years.

BIBLIOGRAPHY

Benson, Clarence H. **Teaching Techniques.** Rev. Ed. Wheaton, IL: Evangelical Teacher Training Association, 1974. Chapter 12.

Edge, Findley B. **Teaching for Results.** Nashville: Broadman Press, 1956. Chapters 12, 13.

Westing, Harold. **Make Your Sunday School Grow Through Evaluation.** Wheaton, IL: Victor Books, 1976.